FROM SUCCESS TO SIGNIFICANCE

Never Underestimate The Competition… Tips to Staying Relevant

by Karen Boyd

COPYRIGHT AND DISCLAIMER

This material is copyright. No part, in whole or in part, may be reproduced by any process, or any other exclusive right exercised, without the permission of DivineResultsCoaching.com © 2018

Karen Boyd, Author

Published by:
Leader Publishing Worldwide
19 Axford Bay
Port Moody, BC V3H 3R4
Tel: 1 888 294 9151
Fax: 1 877 575 9151
Website: www.noresults-nofee.com

DISCLAIMER AND/OR LEGAL NOTICES:
While every attempt has been made to verify information provided in this book, neither the author nor the publisher assumes any responsibility for any errors, omissions or inaccuracies.

Any slights of people or organizations are unintentional. If advice concerning legal or related matters is needed, the services of a qualified professional should be sought. This book is not intended as a source of legal or accounting advice. You should be aware of any laws which govern business transactions or other business practices in your state or province.

The income statements and examples are not intended to represent or guarantee that everyone will achieve the same results. Each individual's success will be determined by his or her desire, dedication, effort, and motivation. There are no guarantees you will duplicate the results stated here, you recognize that any business endeavor has inherent risk for loss of capital.

Any reference to any persons or business, whether living or deceased, existing or defunct, is purely coincidental.

PRINTED IN ST. LOUIS, MO

DEDICATION

I would like to dedicate this book to my number one fan and supporter, my son, Kelvin T. Boyd. As he creates a legacy of his own, a hard-working business owner and mentor to our youth, he is also a dedicated father to his son Kelvin N. Boyd! I admire your strength, tenacity, and dedication to ALL God has assigned to you...Stay In Action!

Karen Boyd

CONTENTS

Chapter 01	...	How to Organize Your Office for Success
Chapter 02	...	Define Your Target Market
Chapter 03	...	Staff Recruitment Training and Development
Chapter 04	...	Systemizing Your Business and Developing Effective Processes
Chapter 05	...	Use Goal Setting Effectively
Chapter 06	...	Copywriting for Profits
Chapter 07	...	How to Create Repeat Business and Have Clients that Pay, Stay and Refer
Chapter 08	...	How to Profit through Time Management
Chapter 09	...	Risk Reversal to Increase Sales
Chapter 10	...	How to Create Newsletters for Your Business, Easily and Quickly

INTRODUCTION

By opening this book you have already taken an important step towards increasing the success of your business. Congratulations in your quest to enhance your business and marketing skills.

Many of the greatest minds of any generation have spent all the time they have left after their achievements desperately pursuing the keys to success, therefore creating financial freedom for a lifetime!

Having achieved such great things, they now sought to share the secret of their successes with the world. After reviewing and refuting many theories in this regard, many have given up without ever truly finding an answer. Others have been left to believe that the secret to financial freedom for life lies within the cards we are dealt or the opportunities we are given. Still, others are of the view that genetics will determine how successful one becomes. But the truth is that none of us were born to be ordinary and people of similar upbringings often do enjoy the same level of success.

The strategies in this book - when strategically implemented with care are guaranteed to make you more money with less effort. Even though I truly believe we are all 1 or 2 great marketing ideas away from more sales opportunities than we can fully imagine, I believe the first two chapters are as important as the following eight. These are strategies that have helped businesses just like yours make hundreds of thousands of dollars - including your competitors...From Success to Significance!

Which happy parents look down at their newborn child and imagine them being just average or just doing enough to get by? None in their right minds of course. We all imagine the great things our children will do, say and accomplish from before they are conceived. And when those children are born, we do all that we can to give them the best possible start to what we hope will be a successful life. Some of these children will be born to parents with great wealth, while others will have to struggle with extremely limited financial resources. But no one knows for sure which of them will become successful. So, what are the keys to living a life of success…becoming significant? Keep reading to learn more!

As you follow the principles in this book, remember it does not matter what industry nor type of business you operate (I've been part of many businesses, both for-profit and non-profit). What matters is that you grasp the heart of the principles, the underlying lessons and strategies, that can help grow any operation in any category of business imaginable.

The best time to start is NOW, not tomorrow, not next week or next year.

Stay In Action,

Karen Boyd

PS. If you would like to arrange a meeting to get a profitable third-party perspective on your business, please send an email to info@divineresultscoaching.com and we will gladly point you in the right direction.

To learn how to avoid the 3 key mistakes all small business owners make, visit www.divineresultsbusinessacademy.com

1

How to Organize Your Office for Success

Have you ever tried to cook a fancy gourmet dinner in a messy kitchen?

It starts out okay. I have all the ingredients I need; it just takes me a little longer to find them as I go. I have to find and clear some counter space, then wipe the crumbs off of it and grab a knife.

Some pots are clean, so I use them first. But then I need the double boiler, and it's still crusted with last night's meal, so I have to wash it. While I'm washing the pot, the garlic and onion that I'm sautéing starts to burn, so I have to run over and rescue it.

Pretty soon, I'm running around like crazy, trying to rescue each item I cook because I'm busy preparing what I need for the next dish. It should be no surprise that the meal was a disaster.

Your place of work is just like your kitchen. It needs to be clean, well-organized, and ready to function. Your tools need to be prepared and ready to go in order to support the tasks you and your staff need to complete.

A well set-up office – with all the necessary tools – will save you time and the expense of redundancy. This is the first key to an effective and successful business operation.

Create an Office for Profitability

Most people understand the relationship between time management and profitability. Effective time management increases productivity; more work can be completed in less time, with less distraction and waste.

Office organization also affects profitability and productivity. A tidy and well-structured office is not only a more pleasant place to work, but it also reduces the time anyone might spend looking for items and digging through loose paperwork.

A well-organized office also encourages better internal communication. There are clear areas of the business that are designated for sales news, target tracking, and project planning. This fosters team building and collaborative work ethic.

Getting Started: Workspace Audit

The best place to start is by taking an honest inventory of the current state of your office or working environment. With that information, you can determine what areas need to be improved, streamlined, or de-cluttered. Spend some time taking a look around your office and note the following:

- Is there a location where internal company information is displayed?
- What is the distance between your office and the printer or photocopier?
- How much lose paper is found around the office?
- What is hung up on the walls?
- Do your staff members have organization systems for their own desks?
- What can be found on your desk?
- How many files are used on a daily or weekly basis?
- Where are old or outdated files kept?

Organize Your Desk

Presumably, your desk is where you spend the most time in your office. It is where you are expected to be the most productive. To get all your important tasks completed.

Simply put, you will be more productive and effective if your workspace is clean and organized. Spend some time each day tidying and organizing your workspace – ideally when you are planning your work or your schedule for the following day.

Here are some other ways you can keep your immediate workspace in the most productive form possible:

Phone. Put your phone on the left side of the desk if you are right handed and on the right side of the desk if you are left handed. Keep a notebook by the phone to record messages and conversation notes. Also, record phone messages here and delete them from your system.

Personal Items. Keep personal items out of your immediate line of sight. Pictures can be distracting, and points for daydreaming.

Organizer. Keep your tablet, smart phone, or Day-timer easily accessible on your desk. Use either one as your main system for notes, tasks, follow-up, and brainstorming. Keep the rest of your desk clear.

Files. Only keep the files you need on your desk or within arm's reach. Store any files you don't use daily or weekly in a filing cabinet further away. You may also maintain your files electronically via OneDrive, GoogleDrive, and/or Dropbox.

Inbox and action items. Sort items in your inbox into an easily accessible file sorter or a stack of paper trays. Separate paper into the following categories: to-do, to-review, waiting response, on-hold, to file.

Organize Your Office

Take the information you gathered in your workplace audit and identify opportunities for improvement. Can the office benefit from a better layout? A paper management system? More clearly defined areas? A new filing system?

The answer will depend on the unique needs of your business, and take into account how you and your staff use the space. Here are some suggestions and guidelines for improving the organization of your office or place of business:

Establish Clear Areas

Divide your office into areas of productivity, and locate all related materials and equipment in each area.

Here are some sample areas you may wish to consider:

- Printing and photocopying
- Office supplies
- Financial paperwork and accounting
- Team gathering
- Kitchen or food-related preparation
- Reception
- Point of sale

Create a Central Location for Information

Many people – including your employees – learn and interpret information that is visual better than any other means of communication. A central location in your office for staff to go for company information and updates is an essential tool for team building and internal communications.

Every office needs:

Whiteboard

Place a whiteboard in an easily accessed place – your staff communication center or the boardroom. This whiteboard is for brainstorming, project planning, marketing planning, or any other use that may be required.

This is a great tool for team meetings, client meetings, and management meetings. The facilitator can diagram information and work through issues on the spot.

Sales Board

Create a customized sales board for your business. Take a whiteboard, and some thin black tape, and create a chart or diagram that records regular sales statistics and targets.

You may wish to separate the whiteboard into two sections – target sales and actual sales, and compare based on weekly, quarterly, and yearly targets. You can also compare actual sales for the same period from the previous year.

12-Month Marketing Planner

Chart your marketing plan on a large calendar and post it in a central area. This is a clear reminder of the big picture, and each of the promotions you have planned over the course of the year.

Remember to write in dry-erase marker so you can easily make changes. Consider color-coding your promotions or projects for easy visibility.

Manage Paper + Filing

System	Steps
Create a master filing system and color code it	Group vendor files (accounts payable) and assign a color Group client files (accounts receivable) and assign a color Group project or product files and assign a color
Sort each filing category by date or alphabetically by name	Sort vendor or supplier files by name Sort client files by client number or name Sort project files by project number or name
Create a binder of master lists for regularly accessed information	Office passwords Financial accounts Goals Birthdays Vendor contact information
Use a bound notebook	Keep track of phone calls and messages Put the date on each page Eliminate loose notepaper
Get rid of magazines and other reading material	Throw away industry magazines and newspapers Keep relevant articles of interest Sort them into files, if necessary
Keep tax-related documents in one spot	File all receipts, donations and other tax related information in the same filing cabinet Make copies of documents you need to file in more than one spot
Create a business care management system	Throw away old business cards Organize cards by last name or company name in a binder or rolodex Enter the information in a data management program, then throw away the cards

2

Define Your Target Market

What is a Target Market?

Many businesses can't answer the question: *Who is your target market?* They have often made the fatal assumption that *everyone* will want to purchase their product or service with the right marketing strategy.

A target market is simply the group of customers or clients who will purchase a specific product or service. This group of people all have something in common, often age, gender, hobbies, or location.

Your target market, then, are the people who will buy your offering. This includes both existing and potential customers, all of whom are motivated to do one of three things:

- Fulfill a need
- Solve a problem
- Satisfy a desire

To build, maintain, and grow your business, you need to know who your customers are, what they do, what they like, and why they would buy your product or service. Getting this wrong – or not taking the time to get it right – will cost you time, money, and potentially the success of your business.

The Importance of Knowing Your Target Market

Knowledge and understanding of your target market is the keystone in the arch of your business. Without it, your product or service positioning, pricing, marketing strategy, and eventually, your business could very quickly fall apart.

If you don't intimately know your target market, you run the risk of making mistakes when it comes to establishing pricing, product mix, or service packages. Your marketing strategy will lack direction and produce mediocre results at best. Even if your marketing message and unique selling proposition (USP) are clear, and your brochure is perfectly designed, it means nothing unless it arrives in the hands (or ears) of the right people.

Determining your target market takes time and careful diligence. While it often starts with a best guess, assumptions cannot be relied on and research is required to confirm original ideas. Your target market is not always your ideal market.

Once you build an understanding of who your target market is, keep up with your market research. Having your finger on the pulse of their motivations and drivers – which naturally change – will help you to anticipate needs or wants and evolve your business.

Types of Markets

Consumer

The Consumer Market includes those general consumers who buy products and services for personal use, or for use by family and friends. This is the market category you or I fall into when we're shopping for groceries or clothes, seeing a movie in the theatre, or going out for lunch. Retailers focus on this market category when marketing their goods or services.

Institutional

The Institutional Market serves society and provides products or services for the benefit of society. This includes hospitals, non-profit organizations, government organizations, schools and universities. Members of the Institutional Market purchase products to use in the provision of services to people in their care.

Business to Business (B2B)

The B2B Market is just what it seems to be: businesses that purchase the products and services of other business to run their operations. These purchases can include products that are used to manufacture other products (raw or technical), products that are needed for daily operations (such as office supplies), or services (such as accounting, shredding, and legal).

Reseller

This market can also be called the "Intermediary Market" because it consists of businesses that act as channels for goods and services between other markets. Goods are purchased and sold for a profit – without any alterations. Members of this market include wholesalers, retailers, resellers, and distributors.

Determining Your Target Market

Product / Service Investigation

The process for determining your target market starts by examining exactly what your offering is, and what the average customer's motivation for purchasing it is. Start by answering the following questions:

Does your offering meet a basic need?	
Does your offering serve a particular want?	
Does your offering fulfill a desire?	
What is the lifecycle of your product / service?	
What is the availability of your offering?	
What is the cost of the average customer's purchase?	
How many times or how often will customers purchase your offering?	

Do you foresee any upcoming changes in your industry or region that may affect the sale of your offering (positive/negative)?	

Market Investigation

- **On the ground.** Spend some time on the ground researching who your target market might be. If you're thinking about opening a coffee shop, hang out in the neighborhood at different times of the day to get a sense of the people who live, work, and play in the neighborhood. Notice their age, gender, clothing, and any other indications of income and activities.

- **At the competition.** Who is your direct competitor targeting? Is there a small niche that is being missed? Observing the clientele of your competition can help to build understanding of your target market, regardless of whether it is the same or opposite. For example, if you own a children's clothing boutique and the majority of middle-class mothers shop at the local department store, you may wish to focus on higher-income families as your target market.

- **Online.** Many cities and towns – or at least regions – have demographic information available online. Research the ages, incomes, occupations, and other key pieces of information about the people who live in the area you operate your business. From this data, you will gain an understanding of the size of your total potential market.

- **With existing customers.** Talk to your existing customers through focus groups or surveys. This is a great way to gather demographic and behavioral information, as well as genuine feedback about product or service quality and other information that will be useful in a business or marketing strategy.

Who is Your Market?

Based on your product / service and market investigations, you will be able to piece together a basic picture of your target market, and some of their general characteristics. Record some notes here. At this point, you may wish to be as specific as possible, or maintain some generalities. You can further segment your market in the next section.

Consumer Target Market Framework

Market Type:	Consumer
Gender:	☐ Male ☐ Female
Age Range:	
Purchase Motivation:	☐ Meet a Need ☐ Serve a Want ☐ Fulfill a Desire
Activities:	
Income Range:	
Marital Status:	
Location:	☐ Neighborhood ☐ City ☐ Region ☐ Country
Other Notes:	

Institutional Target Market Framework

Market Type:	Institutional
Institution Type:	☐ Hospital ☐ Non-profit ☐ School ☐ University ☐ Charity ☐ Government ☐ Church
Purchase Motivation:	☐ Operational Need ☐ Client Want ☐ Client Desire
Purpose of Institution:	
Institution's Client Base:	
Size:	
Location:	☐ Neighborhood ☐ City ☐ Region ☐ Country
Other Notes:	

B2B Target Market Framework

Market Type:	Business to Business (B2B)
Company Size:	
Number of Employees:	

Purchase Motivation:	☐ Operations Need ☐ Strategy ☐ Functionality
Annual Revenue:	
Industry:	
Location(s):	
Purpose of Business:	
People, Culture & Values:	
Other Notes:	

Reseller Target Market Framework

Market Type:	Reseller
Industry:	
Client Base:	
Purchase Motivation:	☐ Operations Need ☐ Client Wants ☐ Functionality

Annual Revenue:	
Age:	
Location:	☐ Neighborhood ☐ City ☐ Region ☐ Country
Other Notes:	

Your Target Market: Putting It Together

Based on the information you gather from your product / service and market investigations, you should have a clear vision of your realistic target market. Here are a few examples of how this information is put together and conclusions are drawn:

Target Market Sample 1: Consumer Market

Business: Baby Clothing Boutique	**Business Purpose:** *Meet a need* (provide clothing for infants and children aged 0 to 5 years) *Serve a want* (clothing is brand name only, and has a higher price point than the competition)
Market Type: Consumer	
Gender: Women	
Marital Status: Married	
Market Observations: located on Main Street of Anytown, a street that is seeing many new boutiques open, proximate to the main shopping mall two blocks from popular mid-	**Industry Predictions:** large number of new housing developments in the city and surrounding areas two new schools in construction expect to see an influx of new

range restaurant that is busy at lunch	families move to town from anycity
Competition Observations: baby clothing also available at two local department stores, and one second-hand shop on opposite sides of town	**Online Research:** half of Anytown's population is female, and 25% have children under the age of 15 years Anytown's population is expected to increase by 32% within three years The average household income for Anytown is $75,000 annually

TARGET MARKET:

The target market can then be described as married mothers with children under five years old, between the ages of 25 and 45, who have recently moved to Anytown from anycity, and have a household income of at least $100K annually.

Target Market Sample 2: B2B Market

Business: Confidential Paper Shredding	**Target Business Size:** Small to medium
Market Type: B2B (Business to Business)	**Target Business Revenue:** $500K to $1M
Business Purpose: *Meet an operations need* (provide confidential on-site shredding services for business documents)	**Target Business Type:** produce or handle a variety of sensitive paper documentation accountants, lawyers, real estate agents, etc.
Market Observations: there are two main areas of office buildings and industrial	**Industry Predictions:** the professional sector is seeing revenue growth of 24% over last

warehouses in anycity three more office towers are being constructed, and will be completed this year	year, which indicates increased client billing and staff recruitment
Competition Observations: one confidential shredding company serves the region, covering anycity and the surrounding towns provide regular (weekly or biweekly) service, but does not have the capacity to handle large volumes at one time	**Online Research:** anycity's biggest employment sectors are: manufacturing, tourism, food services, and professional services

TARGET MARKET:

The target market can then be described as small to medium sized businesses in the professional sector with an annual revenue of $500K to $1M who require both regular and infrequent large volume paper shredding services.

Segmenting Your Market

Your market segments are the groups within your target market – broken down by a determinant in one of the following four categories:

- Demographics
- Psychographics
- Geographics
- Behaviors

Segmenting your target market into several more specific groups allows you to further tailor your marketing campaign and more specifically position your product or service. You may wish to divide your ad campaign into four sections, and target four specific markets with messages that will most resonate with the audience.

For example, the baby clothing store may choose to segment its target market by psychographics, or lifestyle. If the larger target market is *married females with children under five, between the ages of 25 and 45, who have a household income of at least $100K annually*, it can be broken down into the following lifestyle segments:

- Fitness-oriented mothers
- Career-oriented mothers
- New mothers

With these three categories, unique marketing messages can be created that speak to the hot-buttons of each segment. The more accurate and specific you can make communications with your target market, the greater impact you will have on your revenues.

Market Segmentation Variables

Demographic	Psychographic	Geographic	Behavioristic
Age	Personality	Region	Brand Loyalty
Income	Lifestyle	Country	Product Usage
Gender	Values	City	Purchase
Generation	Attitude	Area	Frequency
Nationality	Motivation	Neighborhood	Profitability
Ethnicity	Activities	Density	Readiness to Buy

Marital Status Family Size Occupation Religion Language Education Employment Type Housing Type Housing Ownership Political Affiliation	Interests	Climate	User Status

Understanding Your Target Market

Once you have determined who your market is, make a point of learning everything you can about them. You need to have a strong understanding of who they are, what they like, where they shop, why they buy, and how they spend their time. Remind yourself that you may *think* you know your market, but until you have verified the information, you'll be driving your marketing strategy blind.

Also, be aware that markets change, just like people. Just because you knew your market when you started your business 10 years ago, doesn't mean you know it now. Regular market research is part of any successful business plan, and a great habit to start.

Types of Market Research

Surveys

The simplest way to gather information from your clients or target market is through a survey. You can craft a questionnaire full of questions about your product, service, market demographics, buyer motivations, and so on. Plus, anonymous surveys will produce the most accurate information since names are not attached to the results or specific comments.

Depending on the purpose—whether it is to gather demographic information, product or service feedback, or other data—there are several ways to administer a survey.

1. *Telephone*

   Telephone surveys are a more time-consuming option but have the benefit of live communication with your target market. Generally, it is best to have a third party conduct this type of survey to gather the most honest feedback. This is the method that market researchers use for polling, which is highly reliable.

2. *Online*

   Online surveys are the easiest to administer yourself. There are many web-based services that quickly and easily allow you to custom create your survey and send it to your email marketing list. These services can also analyze, summarize and interpret the results on your behalf. Keep in mind that the results include only those who are motivated to respond, which may slant your results.

3. *Paper-based.*

   Paper surveys are seldom used and can prove to be an inefficient method. Like online surveys, your results are based on the feedback of those who were motivated for one reason or another to respond. However, the time and effort involved in taking the survey, filling it out, and returning it to your place of business may deter people from participating.

Keep in mind that surveys can be complex to administer, and consume more time and resources than you have planned. If you have the budget, consider hiring a professional market research firm to lead or assist with the process. This will also ensure that the methodology is standard practice and will garner the most accurate results.

Website Analysis

Tracking your website traffic is an excellent way to research your existing and potential customer's interests and behavior. From this information, you can ensure the design, structure and content of your website is catering to the people who use it – and the people you want to use it.

User-friendly website traffic analytics programs can easily show you who is visiting your site, where they are from, and what pages of your site they are viewing. Services like Google Analytics can tell you what page they arrive at, where they click to, how much time they spend on each page, and on which page they leave the site.

This is powerful (and free!) information to have in your market research, and easy to monitor monthly or weekly, depending on the needs of your business.

Customer Purchase Data (Consumer Behavior)

If you do not have the budget to conduct your own professional market research, you can use existing resources on consumer behavior. While this data may not be specific to your region or city, general consumer research is actual data that can be helpful in confirming assumptions you may have made about your target market.

Your customer loyalty program or Point of Sale system may also be of help in tracking customer purchases and identifying trends in purchase behavior. If you can track who is buying, what they're buying and how often they're buying, you'll have an arsenal of powerful insight into your existing client base.

Focus Groups

Focus groups look at the psychographic and behavioristic aspects of your target market. Groups of six to 12 people are gathered and asked general and specific questions about their purchase motivations and behaviors. These questions could relate to your business in particular, or to the general industry.

Focus group sessions can also be time consuming to organize and facilitate, so consider hiring the services of a professional market research firm. You may also receive more honest information if a third party is asking the questions and receiving the responses from focus group participants.

For cost savings, consider partnering with an associate in the same industry who is not a direct competitor, and who would benefit from the same market data.

3

Staff Recruitment Training and Development

The people you hire to work for your business can be your biggest assets and your biggest headaches. They can support and help you to achieve the vision you have for your company – but they can also prevent you from reaching that vision.

Too many businesses overlook the role of employee recruitment and retention when planning for the success of their organization. Staffing is an important exercise that needs to be purpose driven and strategic, just like marketing.

It is vital to understand in today's market that the relationship between employee and employer is a two-way street. Now, more than ever, employees have a "what's in it for me?" attitude that extends beyond salary and benefits expectations into incentive and rewards programs. The days of simple compensation structures are over.

Now, this may sound like a big headache, but it's actually a good thing! With some simple systems and open dialogue, you will be able to effectively create – and keep – your dream team.

The Power of Your Dream Team

How much of your own personal time has human resources – staff hiring, firing, management issues, etc. – has taken this year? No doubt staff recruitment and retention is one of the biggest challenges facing any business owner today.

The truth is, if you spent half as much time on human resources as you do on marketing, I guarantee your sales would increase dramatically.

Customers know the difference between happy employees and disgruntled ones, and it makes a difference when it comes to purchase decisions. Would you rather have your car serviced by a grumpy mechanic who doesn't feel his good work is rewarded, or a pleasant one who just stepped out a weekly team meeting?

A successful business owner has confidence in the people who work for him, because he believes they are the best people for the job. Employees who know their employer believes in their skills and abilities will go over and above to get the job done, to make the sale.

Successful business owners invest time and money in finding and keeping the right people. These are the people who share and support the collective vision for the company.

I'm not talking about a complicated formula, or magic concoction. I'm talking about some careful thought and a proactive strategy that will make your business shine from the inside out.

Finding Your Dream Employees

Building a dream team starts by finding and hiring the right people for the job. Sounds simple enough. You post an ad, find someone who has the necessary qualifications, and hire them on.

Not so fast. Recruitment is a complex process that can dramatically impact your business operations. Just like finding and securing the right customers, finding and hiring the right candidates requires pro-active planning and careful evaluation.

If you currently work with a recruiting agency to build your team, now may be a good time to stop and evaluate the effectiveness of their service. While a recruiting agency can save you the time and hassle of working through the hiring process, it can also cost more money in the long run.

I always recommend creating an internal recruitment system, not because recruiting agencies do a bad job, but because no one knows your business like you do.

An internal recruitment system ensures that the true essence of your business culture is communicated – from advertisement to interview. You also have the opportunity to communicate expectations from the outset, instead of relying on the recruiter to relay this information. The middle-man's thoughts and impressions are eliminated, leaving you to make decisions based on your impression of the candidate and no one else's.

Step One: Advertise the Opportunity

The first step in recruiting candidates is obviously letting potential candidates know about the opportunity with your company.

But before you pick up the phone to place a classified ad, remember that advertising for potential employees requires just as much consideration and planning as general advertising for your business.

You need to ask yourself:

- Who is your ideal candidate?
- What are their skills and qualifications?
- What is their personality or demeanor?
- What are they passionate about?
- What are they looking for in a job?

Once you have a mental picture of your candidate, then you can begin to write an ad that will not only reach them, but also inspire them to act (and apply).

When writing this ad, be as specific as possible and focus on the benefits of the job. Remember that potential candidates screen job postings with an eye for "what's in it for me." Tell them exactly that.

Here are a few sample job postings:

Are you the Marketing Assistant we need?

About You

You're fun, friendly and have a keen eye for detail. You're always two steps ahead of your colleagues, and eager to take on new and exciting challenges.

You'll be the glue that keeps the marketing team operating in a seamless fashion, responsible for website updates, copywriting, event coordination and client relations. You'll be punctual, responsible, and well put together.

You'll ideally have an undergraduate degree in marketing or English, and some previous office experience, but a fast learner with a great attitude will also get our attention.

About Us

We are a collaborate team of young professionals. We offer a competitive salary, great benefits and performance incentives.

Think you fit the bill? Email your resume and cover letter to John Smith at jsmith@email.com by Friday at 4pm.

Are Computers Your Life?

About You

You are smart, outgoing, and a wiz when it comes to computer programming. You're on your friend's speed dial for computer emergencies, large and small. Helping people understand the complex digital world is your passion.

You'll be our Lead Computer Technician, managing our computer repair counter and five Junior Technicians. You'll have great people skills, mounds of patience, and enjoy working as part of a dynamic team.

About Us

We operate Anytown's leading computer repair store and are known across the region for our customer service. We work hard, play hard, and offer a competitive benefits package to our employees.

Tell us why this job is for you. Email your resume and cover letter to info@computerworld.com by Thursday, September 23.

Both job postings speak directly to a very targeted audience. They're friendly, colloquial, and communicate the job requirements in an informal way.

Every job posting should:

- Be colloquial (written in the way that you talk)
- Be specific
- Describe benefits
- Include skills, qualifications, duties and job title
- Be written in the present tense
- Have a great headline
- Call the reader to action
- Be simple – in word choice and sentence structure
- Be more exciting than the competition

Now that you have a great ad to post, you need to decide where you are going to publish it. This depends on the level of the job (junior to management) and on the specific type of candidate you are looking to recruit.

Here are the five major places to advertise your opportunity:

Government Employment Center

These are great places to find blue-collar or junior level employees. Candidates register with the center, which keeps their resumes on file. Be cautious with this route – it can produce a wide variety of candidates who are not qualified.

Local Newspaper

This is a great place to post junior to mid-level employment opportunities. You're looking for basic qualifications from local applicants, perhaps even for part-time positions, with minimal cost.

Regional or City Newspaper

Senior employment opportunities that require specific high-level qualifications are best advertised with a broad scope. This incurs a greater cost but will return a greater variety of candidates.

Online

This is a cheap way to tap into a massive database of job seekers. Post your ad online on sites like www.monster.com or www.workopolis.com and watch the resumes come flooding in. Many highly qualified job seekers who do not wish to register with a recruitment agency will use these services.

Referrals

The most ideal way to find candidates is through your existing network – including associates, colleagues, employees, friends and family. These candidates come to you already vetted by a trusted source. You may also wish to consider giving your staff an incentive to refer their qualified friends and associates to you.

You should also brainstorm a list of any other niche areas that your target market may look for a job. Consider industry publications, industry associations, small publications, etc.

Once you've posted your ad, your next step is to manage the inquiries that come flooding in.

Step Two: Screen Candidates

This is one of the most time-consuming aspects of the recruitment process, so you will need to work out a system to manage the response to your job posting.

A structured interview process will ensure that you ask all potential candidates the same questions and provide them with the same information about the role as well as about your company.

1. Decide whether all inquiries will be handled by one person or several. This will depend on your staff resources and capacity. A system will allow multiple employees to assist in the process.

For example, if your candidates have been instructed to submit their resume and cover letter to you through email, designate a single email address and inbox to receiving and responding. This way you or another staff member will not be bombarded by emails and can designate an hour of time each day to managing the inquiries. If your candidates are calling in, designate a unique phone number or answering machine to handle this task.

2. Decide how inquiries will be responded to. This can be as simple as an email acknowledging receipt of the resume, or specific instructions on an answering machine. Ensure everyone receives the same information, and that you receive the same level of information from all candidates (resume, cover letter, portfolio, references, and other relevant information.).

If you have asked candidates to call you instead of submitting their resumes through email, create a standard checklist of questions to ask them, as well as of information to provide them with. You may wish to create a script. Some questions might include:

- What kind of job are you looking for?
- Why do you think you would be well suited for this position?
- Tell me a bit about yourself.
- What makes you interested in our company?

Use this opportunity to get a feel for the applicant's personality and trust your initial impression. Create a form on which to record this information, and file it with their resume when you receive it.

3. Devise a process for reviewing resumes or applications. The easiest and most time efficient way to do this is in a single session, after the stated deadline, and not as you receive them. You may wish to enlist the assistance of a senior colleague to provide a second opinion.

Review the resumes and application materials, and divide the applications into three piles: interview, no interview, and maybe. From here you can begin to call candidates and set up a first interview.

It is also a good idea to be in touch with unsuccessful candidates, and politely let them know that you will not be asking them in for an interview. If you anticipate your response rate will be overwhelming, you may wish to consider stating in your advertisement that only successful applicants will be called.

Step Three: First Interview

The first interview is also a screening interview; your objective is to develop a first impression of the candidate as a person, and to determine if they are qualified for the position. If you feel you have found an ideal candidate, this is also your opportunity to convince them to choose your company over any others they may be considering. Good people don't stay in the market long.

Interview Structure

You will need to decide on a structure, or system, for the interview process as well. Will you be conducting the first interviews, or will another manager? Will the interviews be conducted one on one, or will several employees participate? If you are replacing an employee, you may want to consider inviting that employee into the interview to provide insight into the role.

Interview Materials

Just as you are asking the potential candidate to come prepared to the interview, you must be as well.

- Have an outline prepared of what you would like to cover. Topics include: company history, job description, interview questions, compensation structure, availability, and room for advancement.
- Bring two copies of a typed job description. Include all tasks the candidate will be responsible for completing or assisting with.
- A company profile or overview document (other marketing collateral will also work here).

Interview Attitude

Begin to build a relationship with each applicant. The purpose of the interview is not just to discuss the job description, or for the applicant to get all the interview questions "right." It is to determine if this person has the right attitude for the job, and whether they will fit in with the company's culture and its employees.

Keep the interview professional, but make sure the applicant is comfortable. Interviews test our ability to perform under pressure, but you will want to gain an understanding of the applicant's true nature. Remember that even if the applicant is not well suited to the role they have applied for, they may be suited to a future opportunity with the company.

Interview Questions

The questions you decide to ask the candidate are highly specific to your company and the role you are hiring for. Take some time to brainstorm what you really need to know about each person, and what questions you can ask to get that information.

Keep in mind that part of the objective of the first interview is to get a sense of the candidate's personality. You will want to ask questions about their responses and begin to establish a real relationship with them.

Here are some starter interview questions to get you going:

- Tell me a little bit about your background.
- What has been your first impression of our company/product/services?
- Tell me about a time when… [insert a likely scenario they will encounter in the position]. How did it make you feel? How did you handle the situation?
- What advantages do you feel you have over the other candidates?
- What are your strengths? Weaknesses?
- Tell me about an achievement you're proud of.
- Why did you leave your last position?
- Where do you see yourself in five years?
- …and so on.

Make sure you take good notes or ask a junior member of your team to take notes for you. Also record your impression of the candidate after each interview. You will want to be able to reflect on each interview before inviting the candidate to the next phase of the selection process.

When the first interviews have been completed, review your notes and discuss your first impressions with other employees involved in the process. Then, decide who you would like to invite back for a second interview, and let the unsuccessful candidates know they are not right for this role.

Step Four: Second Interview + Reference Check

The second interview is used to confirm your impressions of the applicants you believe are well suited for the job. It can also be used to get more information, or to more closely compare two solid candidates.

Make sure you only offer a second interview to those you are considering hiring. If you are on the fence about a candidate, chances are your instincts are right, and bringing them in for a second interview is a waste of their time and yours.

Callbacks

When you call a candidate to invite them to come in for a second interview, remain professional and don't make any allusions to a job offer. If your impression of them changes during the second interview, you do not want to have to go back on something you said. Let them know what you thought of them based on the first interview and ask if they would be interested in meeting with you a second time.

Give yourself and the candidate a day or two between interviews to reflect on the first interview and prepare for the second.

Interviewer

You may wish to change the person or team of people who conducted the first interview. Usually the second interview is conducted with more senior team members at the table.

Interview Questions

While the second interview is often less structured than the first – a relationship has already begun to be established – you should still prepare a list of questions for the candidate.

These questions should focus on the specific tasks related to the job, and on providing more information about the culture, systems, and values of the company. You can also use the second interview to ask questions you may not have had the chance to in the first interview.

Office Tour + Introductions

Once you have determined that you have found the candidate for the job, take them on a tour of your office or business, and introduce them to your staff members. This is a good way gaining an initial understanding of how the candidate might interact with your existing staff members.

Calling References

This is the final – arguably most important – step to make before offering the job to the candidate. You should ask your candidate for at least three employment references, and perhaps one character reference.

Contact each reference, explain who you are and why you are calling. Then ask if they have a few moments to answer some questions about the candidate. You will want to find out information about punctuality, professionalism, skills, and their reason for leaving. Cross reference this information with your interview notes to ensure consistency between the candidate and their reference.

Step Five: Hire Your Employee

Provided their references are solid, now is the time to make them an offer of employment.

Call the candidate personally to offer them the job. Make sure you congratulate them and express your enthusiasm in welcoming them into your team. You will also need to follow up your conversation with a letter or email that includes the job offer document or contract.

In the case where a candidate declines the job offer, you may wish to do a reference check on your second pick and make them an offer.

Good luck!

Training Your Dream Employees

Once you have landed your dream employees through a rigorous recruitment process, it is essential that you continue to invest in your decision by putting them through a thorough training process.

Training is an element of recruitment. A new employee's orientation and training sets the tone for their entire employment; this includes their impression of your business, its systems, and respect for its leaders. This has an impact on your ability to retain good people and avoid unnecessary or redundant recruitment processes.

Too often, businesses rely on junior employees to train new ones without any guidelines or 'curriculum.' New employees are thrown into the deep end without clear expectations or an understanding of 'how things are done around here.'

These elements affect how an employee perceives their own required level of effort or performance. A business that doesn't give much thought to planning, expectations, and preparation will end up showing a new employee that the same lack of attention is expected from them.

Here are some things to ensure you implement when you create your comprehensive training system:

Prior Learning / Existing Knowledge

Acknowledge your new employee's prior learning, and don't overestimate or underestimate their existing knowledge.

Choice of Trainer

Make sure the person or people who will be training the new employee are sufficiently qualified and experienced. If an administrator is leading a salesperson's training and orientation, consider asking another salesperson or more senior team member to assist on specific days or sessions.

Training Materials

Have all the required training materials handy. This includes company manuals, industry guidebooks, common reference materials, work samples and anything else that will aid in the training efforts.

Training Tools

Also ensure you have the tools available to train your new hire. Will the training be held at their workstation, or another workstation? Do you have all the software you need? All the equipment required? Doing so will ensure the training runs smoothly and the time provided will be used effectively.

Time

Provide more than ample time for training – including time for questions and elaboration. Rushing training benefits no one, including your profits.

Testing

Consider including some 'tests' or checks to ensure the new hire understands each component of the training. Ask the trainer and the trainee to sign-off on each section.

The Big Picture

Each team member's role is part of a larger picture: the company as a whole. Ensure that the trainee understands how their role contributes to the big picture on each level. If they are a junior member of a department, they should understand how their job contributes to the department, as well as how the department contributes to the entire company.

Feedback

The trainee should be able to ask questions and review information at any time – including after the training process. Create an environment that encourages open dialogue and encourages employees to ask questions when they are unsure of a task.

The other common mistake that many companies make is ending training after the first few weeks of a new hire's employment.

Training is an ongoing process for every single member of your team, and there should be a system or structure in place to ensure that staff training and development happens on a regular basis. This can include cross-training, employee development, and new systems orientation. Regular training not only benefits your staff and improves their performance, but it allows you – the business owner – to:

- Implement new policies + procedures
- Invest in your staff, thereby improving confidence and morale
- Evaluate staff performance at an individual and team level
- Reward staff based on performance improvements
- Provide a regular arena for feedback and discussion, including positive and negative experiences and issues

One-on-One Training + Evaluation

An effective system of ongoing training is weekly, monthly, or quarterly staff reviews. When conducted one-on-one, this provides a forum for regular communication with employees to review performance and identify areas for improvement. A one-on-one environment will encourage more open and honest dialogue than if the session were conducted as part of a team.

As a business owner, these sessions are valuable sources of information and insight into the strengths, weaknesses and motivations of your team.

If you have a large staff, consider pairing junior staff with senior staff and establishing mentorship relationships. This is a powerful way to build the synergy of your team and frees you up from weekly meetings with each staff member. Instead, each senior staff member can report back to you on the results of their regular training sessions, and you only need to conduct these sessions with your senior staff.

Team Training

Team training events are great team builders and provide insight into how your team interacts as a whole. These can take the form of "lunch and learns," where senior staff or guest speakers conduct an hour-long session with staff members, or more social team building exercises with a less formal program.

Team training exercises will shed light on the leaders and followers in an organization and bring together employees who may work outside of the office. These can be especially helpful if you and your senior staff do not see the team 'in action' on a daily basis.

Keeping Your Dream Employees

Now that you have spent hours of time and potentially hundreds or thousands of dollars recruiting and training your staff, your human resource job is done, right?

I suppose you've done what you've set out to do: get the right people working for you. But what happens when those people get bored? Or stolen by another company? Or feel they've "done all they can do" at your company?

The final step in the overall recruitment process is employee retention. This includes keeping your employees happy, supporting their development, and giving them incentive to continuously improve their performance.

Environment

The environment you create for your staff has a huge impact on your employee retention rates. This includes the interior design and layout of your office or business, the lighting, plants, and kitchen amenities available. It also includes the culture of the company – what is the general working atmosphere? Are most people loud? Quiet? Is there a buzz or hum to the office space?

The bottom line is that employees should enjoy and feel comfortable coming to their workplace – they do spend most of their waking hours there.

Spending a little more on comfortable office furniture and amenities like coffee, tea, snacks and social spaces will go a long way toward keeping your employees happy at work.

Recognition, Rewards, and Incentive Programs

Did you know that many employees place more value on positive public recognition for a job well done than they do on salary?

Recognition and rewards are powerful tools when it comes to keeping employees happy. Positive feedback from those in more senior positions has a higher perceived value than a 3-5% salary increase – and it costs the business little to nothing to implement.

Incentive programs are a formalized way of rewarding employees for their achievements and successes. Clear targets and milestones are identified, and when an individual or team reaches those milestones they are rewarded with bonuses or prizes.

Recognition, rewards and incentive programs are an important part of employee retention, as well as team building.

Professional Development Programs

Another common reason employees choose to leave their positions is professional development. Many feel they need to move to another company in order to develop their careers or gain more responsibility. They may not necessarily dislike their current role but become bored or stagnated and believe they have 'done all they can do' at that particular company.

Keeping good people means providing opportunities for growth and advancement within your company. This benefits the company because you can hire from within and save money and time on recruiting and training new staff. It also benefits your employee and increases their loyalty toward your business.

Professional development programs are an important part of staff retention – but they are also an important part of business growth and development. A company with staff who are always increasing their knowledge and improving their skills will stay on the 'cutting edge' of their industry and have an advantage over the competition.

Ongoing training and development should be a primary focus for any growing business. Here's why:

- Increases productivity
- Increases staff retention
- Increases workplace safety and morale
- Increases customer service
- Increases sales

Professional development programs typically focus on the big picture ambitions of the company and its staff members. The longer-term goals and career ambitions are recorded and taken into consideration.

Professional development can be easily worked into your ongoing one-on-one training systems. Keep a folder or binder for each staff member that outlines current role responsibilities, short- and long-term goals, and areas for improvement, and review it during your weekly or monthly meetings. Identify specific areas for growth and develop plans of action for that growth.

For example, if your marketing assistant wants to grow into a marketing coordinator or manager role, and needs to improve her people management skills, consider putting her through a management course.

Maintaining this program doesn't have to be a time-consuming task. With some simple system tools and a commitment to regularly scheduled meetings, you can have a clear and effective program for your staff.

- Evolving job description document to monitor role responsibilities and tasks
- Regular performance evaluations
- Goal planning worksheets
- Continuing education programs at local business schools
- Regular meetings between staff and supervisors
- Rewards and incentives

Investing in your staff is key! Hiring the right people, initial & ongoing training, customer service focused, employee incentives, and quality assurance are all key areas of focus.

4

Systemizing Your Business and Developing Effective Processes

One of the biggest mistakes a business owner can make is to create a company that is dependent on the owner's involvement for the success of its daily operations. This is called working "in" your business. You're writing basic sales letters, licking stamps, and guiding staff step-by-step through each task.

There are a number of problems with this approach. One is redundancy. You're paying your staff to carry out tasks that you eventually complete. The second is poor time management. You're spending your day – at your high hourly rate – on tasks as they arise, leaving little room for the tasks you need to be focused on.

However, the biggest issue I have with this approach is that countless intelligent business owners are spending the majority of their time operating their business, instead of *growing* it.

A good test of this is to ask yourself, what would happen if you took off to a hot sunny destination for three weeks and left your cell phone, PDA and laptop at home. Would your business be able to continue operating?

If you said no, then this chapter is for you.

Systemizing your business is about putting policies and procedures in place to make your business operations run smoother – and more importantly – without your constant involvement. With your newfound free time, **you will be able to focus your efforts on the bigger picture: strategically growing your business.**

Why Systemize?

For most small business owners, systems simply mean freedom from the day-to-day functioning of their organization. The company runs smoothly, makes a profit, and provides a high level of service – regardless of the owner's involvement.

Systemizing your business is also a healthy way to plan for the future. You're not going to be working forever – what happens when you retire? How will you transition your business to new ownership or management? How will you take that vacation you've been dreaming of?

Businesses that function without their ownership are also highly valuable to investors. Systemizing your business can position it in a favorable light for purchase and merit a high price tag.

A system is any process, policy, or procedure that consistently achieves the same result, regardless of who is completing the task.

Any task that is performed in your business more than once can be systemized. Ideally, the tasks that are completed on a cyclical basis – daily, weekly, monthly, and quarterly – should be systemized so much so that anyone can perform them.

Systems can take many forms – from manuals and instruction sheets, to signs, banners, and audio or video recordings. They don't have to be elaborate or extensive, just provide enough information in step-by-step form to guide the person performing the task.

Benefits of Business Systems

There are unlimited benefits available to you and your business through systemization. The more systems you can successfully implement, the more benefits you'll see.

- Better cost management
- Improved time management
- Clearer expectations of staff
- More effective staff training and orientation
- Increased productivity (and potentially profits)
- Happier customers (consistent service)

- Maximized conversion rates
- Increased staff respect for your time
- Increased level of individual initiative
- Greater focus on long-term business growth

Taking Stock of Your Existing Systems

The first step in systemizing your business is taking a long look at the existing systems (if any) in your business. At this point, you can look for any systems that have simply emerged as "the way we do things here."

How do your staff answer the phone? What is the process customers go through when dealing with your business? How are employees hired? Trained? How is performance Reviewed and rewarded?

Some of your systems may be highly effective, and not require any changes. Others may be ineffective and require some reworking. If you have previously established some systems, now is a good time to check-in and evaluate how well they are functioning.

Use the following chart to record what systems currently exist in your business.

Existing Systems
Administration

Financials	
Communication	
Customer Relations	
Employees	
Marketing	
Data	

Seven Areas to Systemize

There is no doubt that system creation – especially when none exist to begin with – is a daunting and time-consuming task. For many businesses, it can be difficult to determine where to start to make the best use of their time from the onset.

Here are seven main areas of your business you can to systemize. Begin with one area and move to the other areas as you are ready. Alternately, start with one or two systems within each area, and evaluate how those new systems affect your business. Each business will require its own unique set of systems.

1. Administration

This is an important area of your business to systemize because administrative roles tend to see a high turnover. A series of systems will reduce training time and keep you from explaining how the phones are to be answered each time a new receptionist joins your team.

Administrative Systems	
Opening and closing procedures	Filing and paper management
Phone greeting	Workflow
Mail processing	Document production
Sending couriers	Inventory management
Office maintenance (watering plants, emptying recycle bins, etc.)	Order processing
	Making orders

2. Financials

This is one area of systems that you will need to keep a close eye on – but that doesn't mean you have to do the work yourself. Financial management systems are everything from tracking credit card purchases to invoicing clients and following up on overdue accounts.

These systems will help to prevent employee theft and allow you to always have a clear picture of your numbers. It will allow you to control purchasing and ensure that each decision is signed-off on.

Financial Systems	
Purchasing	Profit / loss statements
Credit card purchase tracking	Invoicing
Accounts payable	Daily cash out
Accounts receivable	Petty cash
Bank deposits	Employee expenses
Cutting checks	Payroll
Tax payments	Commission payments

3. Communications

The area of communication is essential and time consuming for any business. Fax cover letters, sales letters, internal memos, reports, and newsletters are items that need to be created regularly by different people in your organization.

Most of the time, these communications aren't much different from one to the next, yet each are created from scratch by a different person. There is a huge opportunity for systemization in this area of your business. Systemized communication ensures consistency and company differentiation.

Communication Systems	
Internal memo template	Newsletter template
Fax cover template	Sales letter template(s)
Letterhead template	Meeting minutes template
Team meeting agenda	Report template

Sending faxes	Internal meetings
Internal emails	Scheduling

4. Customer Relations

Another important area for systemization is customer relations. This includes everything the customer sees or touches in your company, as well as any interaction they might have with you or your staff members.

Establishing a customer relations system will also ensure that new staff members understand how customers are handled in *your* business. It will allow you to maintain a high level of customer service, without constantly reminding staff of your policies. It will also ensure that the success of your customer relations and retention does not hinge on you or any other individual salesperson.

Customer Relations Systems	
Incoming phone call script	Sales process
Outgoing phone call script	Sales script
Customer service standards	Newsletter templates
Customer retention strategy	Ongoing customer communication
Customer communications templates	strategy
	Customer liaison policy

5. Employees

Create systems in your business for hiring, training, and developing your employees. This will establish clear expectations for the employee and streamline time consuming activities like recruitment.

Employees with clear expectations who work within clear structures are happier and more productive. They are motivated to achieve 'A' when they know they will receive 'B' if they do. Establishing a clear training manual will also save you and your staff the time and hassle of training each new staff member on the fly.

Employee Systems	
Employee recruitment	Staff uniforms or dress code
Employee retention	Employee training
Incentive and rewards program	Ongoing training and professional development
Regular employee reviews	
Employee feedback structure	Job descriptions and role profiles

6. Marketing

This is likely an area in which you spend a large part of your time. You focus on generating new leads and getting more people to call you or walk through your doors. These efforts can be systemized and delegated to other staff members.

Use the information in this program to create simple systems for your basic promotional efforts. Any one of your staff should be able to pick up a marketing manual and implement a successful direct mail campaign or place a purposeful advertisement.

Marketing Systems	
Referral program	Regular advertisements
Customer retention program	Advertisement creation system
Regular promotions	Direct mail system
Marketing calendar	Sales procedures
Enquiries management	Lead management

7. Data

While we like to think we operate a paperless office, often the opposite is true. Your business needs to have clear systems for managing paper and electronic information to ensure that information is protected, easily accessed, and only kept when necessary.

Data management systems help you keep your office organized. Everyone knows where information is to be stored, and how it is to be handled, which prevents big stacks of paper with no place to go.

Ensure that within your data management systems you include a data backup system. That way, if anything happens to your server or computer software, your data – and potentially your business – is protected.

Data Management Systems	
IT Management	Client file system
Data backup	Project file system
Computer repairs	Point of sale system
Electronic information storage	Financial data management

Implementing New Systems

If you completed the exercise earlier in this chapter, you will have a good idea of the systems that are currently in place in your business. The next step is to determine what systems you need to create in your business.

To do this you will need to get a better understanding of the tasks that you and your employees complete on a daily and weekly basis. If you operate a timesheet program, this can be a good source of information. Alternately, ask staff to keep a daily log for a week of all the tasks they contribute to or complete. Doing so will not only give you valuable insight into how they spend their time on a daily basis, but also involve them in the systemizing process.

Review all task logs or timesheet records at the end of the week, remove duplicates, and group like tasks together. From here you can categorize the tasks into business areas like the seven listed above or create your own categories.

Then, you will need to prioritize and plan your system creation and implementation efforts. Choose one from each category, or one category to focus on at a time. The amount you can take on will depend on your business needs, and the staff resources you have available to you for this process.

Remember that system creation is a long-term process – not something that will transform your business overnight. Be patient and focus on the items that hold the highest priority.

Creating Your Systems

There is a big variety of ways you can create systems for your business – depending on the type of system you need and the type of business you operate. Some systems will be short and simple – i.e., a laminated sign in the kitchen that outlines step-by-step how to make the coffee – while others will be more complex – i.e., your sales scripts or letter templates.

One thing all of your systems have in common is steps. There is a linear process involved from start to finish. Begin by writing out each of the steps involved in completing the task and provide as much detail as you can.

Then, review your step-by-step guide with the employee(s) who regularly complete the task and gather their feedback. Once you have incorporated their input, decide what format the system needs to be in: manual, laminated instruction sheet, sign, office memo, etc.

Testing Your Systems

Now that you have created a system, you will need to make sure that it works. More specifically, you need to make sure that it works without your involvement.

Implement the new system for an appropriate period of time – a week or month – then ask for input from staff, suppliers and vendors, and customers. Evaluate if it is informative enough for your staff, seamless enough for your suppliers, and whether it meets or exceeds your customer's needs.

Take that feedback and revise the system accordingly. You will rarely get the system right the first time – so be patient.

Systems will also need to be evaluated and revised on a regular basis to ensure your business processes are kept up to date. Structure an annual or bi-annual review of systems and stick to it.

Employee Buy-In

It will be nearly impossible for you to develop effective systems without the involvement and input of your employees. These are the people who will be using the systems, and who are completing the tasks on a regular basis without systems. They have a wealth of knowledge to assist you in this process.

Employees can also draft the systems for you to review and finalize. This will make the systemization process a much faster and more efficient one.

It is also important to note that when you introduce new systems into your company, there may be a natural resistance to the change. People – including your employees – are habitual people who can become set in the way they are used to doing things.

Delegation

The final step to systemizing your business is delegation. What is the point of creating systems unless someone other than you can use them to perform tasks?

This doesn't have to mean completely removing your involvement from the process, but it does mean giving your employees enough freedom to complete the task within the structure of the systems you have spent time and considerable thought creating.

After that, allow yourself the freedom of focusing on the tasks that you most enjoy, and most deserve – like creating big picture strategies to grow your business, increase your profits, and enjoy more freedom of your time.

5

Use Goal Setting Effectively

We've all heard about the power of setting goals. Everyone has surely seen statistics that connect goal setting to success in both your business life, and your personal life. I'm sure if I asked you today what your goals are, you could rattle off a few wants and hopes without thinking too long.

However, what most people do not realize is that the power of goal setting lies in *writing goals down*. Committing goals to paper and reviewing them regularly gives you a 95% higher chance of achieving your desired outcomes. Studies have shown that only three to five percent of people in the world have written goals – the same three to five percent who have achieved success in business and earned considerable wealth.

These studies have also found that by retirement, only four per cent of people in the world will have enough accumulated wealth to maintain their income level, and quality of life. As a business owner, it is essential that you develop a plan for your retirement, but it is equally essential that you develop a plan for your success.

This chapter focuses on the power of goal setting as part of your business success. We'll teach you to set SMART goals that are rooted in your own personal value system and supporting techniques to achieve your goals faster.

What are Goals?

Goals are clear targets that are attached to a specific time frame and action plan; they focus your efforts and drive your motivation in a clear direction. Goals are different from dreams in that they outline a plan of action, while dreams are a conceptual vision of your wish or desired outcome.

Goals require work; work on yourself, work for your business, and work for others. You cannot achieve a goal – no matter how badly you want it – without being prepared to make a considerable effort. If you are ready to invest your time and energy, goals will help you to:

- Realize a dream or wish for your personal or business life
- Make a change in your life – add positives, or remove negatives
- Improve your skills and performance ability
- Start or change a habit – positive or negative

Why Set Goals?

As we've already reviewed, setting goals and committing them to paper is the most effective way to cultivate success. The most important reason to set a goal is **to attach a clear action plan to a desired outcome.**

Goals help focus our time and energy on one (or several) key outcome at a time. Many business owners have hundreds of ideas whirring around in their heads at any one time, on top of daily responsibilities. By writing down and focusing on a few ideas at a time, you can prioritize and concentrate your efforts, avoid being stretched too thin, and produce greater results.

Since goals attach action to outcomes, goals can help to break down big dreams into manageable (and achievable) sections. Creating a multi-goal strategy will put a road map in place to help you get to your desired outcome. If your goal is to start a pizza business and make six figures a year, there are a number of smaller steps to achieve before you achieve your end result.

Success doesn't happen by itself. It is the result of consistent and committed action by an individual who is driven to achieve something. Success means something different for everyone, so creating goals is a personal endeavor. Goals can be large and small, personal and public, financial and spiritual. It is not the size of the goal that matters; what matters is that you write the goal down and commit to making the effort required to achieve it.

What happens when I achieve a goal?

You should congratulate yourself and your team, of course! By rewarding yourself and your team after every achievement, you not only train your mind to associate hard work with reward, you will also develop loyalty among your employees.

You should also ask yourself if your achievement can be taken to the next level, or if your goal can be stretched by building on the effort you have already made. Consistently setting new and higher targets will lay the framework for constant improvement and personal and professional growth.

Power of Positive Thinking

When was the last time you tuned into your internal stream of consciousness? What does the stream of thoughts that run through your mind sound like? Are they positive? Negative? Are they logical? Reasonable?

Positive thinking and healthy self-talk are the most important business tools you can ever cultivate; by programming a positive stream of subconscious thoughts into your mind, you can control your reality, and ultimately your goals. Think about someone you know who is constantly negative; someone who complains and whines and makes excuses for their unhappiness. How successful are they? How do their fears and doubts become reality in their world?

You are what you continuously believe about yourself and your environment. If you focus your mind on something in your mental world, it will nearly always manifest as reality in your physical world.

Positive thinking is a key part of setting goals. You won't achieve your goal until you believe that you can. You will achieve your goals faster when you believe in yourself, and the people around you who are helping to make your goal a reality.

Successful people are rooted in a strong belief system – belief in themselves, belief in the work they are doing, and belief in the people around them. They are motivated to improve and learn, but also confident in their existing skills and knowledge. Their positive attitude and energy is clearly felt in everything they do.

Ever notice how complainers usually surround themselves with other complainers? The same is true of positive thinkers. If you cultivate an upbeat and positive attitude, you will be surrounded by people who share your values and outlook on life.

Too often, people and our society subscribe to a continuous stream of negative chatter. The more you hear it, the more you'll believe it.

How many times have you heard:

- That's impossible.
- Don't even bother.
- It's already been done.
- We tried that, and it didn't work.
- You're too young.
- You're too old.
- You'll never get there.
- You'll never get that done.
- You can't do that.

Positive thinking and positive influences will provide the support you need to achieve your goals. Choose your friends and close colleagues wisely and surround yourself with positive thinkers.

Creating SMART Goals

SMART goals are just that: smart. Whether you are setting goals for your personal life, your business, or with your employees, goals that have been developed with the SMART principle have a higher probability of being achieved.

The SMART Principle

1. Specific

Specific goals are clearer and easier to achieve than nonspecific goals. When writing down your goal, ask yourself the five "W" questions to narrow down what exactly you are aiming for. Who? Where? What? When? Why?

For example, instead of a nonspecific goal like, "get in shape for the summer," a specific goal would be, "go to the gym three times a week and eat twice as many vegetables."

2. Measurable

If you can't measure your goal, how will you know when you've achieved it? Measurable goals help you clearly see where you are, and where you want to be. You can see change happen as it happens.

Measurable goals can also be broken down and managed in smaller pieces. They make it easier to create an action plan or identify the steps required to achieve your goal. You can track your progress, revise your plan, and celebrate each small achievement. For example, instead of aiming to increase revenue in 2019, you can set out to increase revenue by 30% in the next 12 months and celebrate each 10% along the way.

3. Achievable

Goals that are achievable have a higher chance of being realized. While it is important to think big, and dream big, too often people set goals that are simply beyond their capabilities and wind up disappointed. Goals can stretch you, but they should always be feasible to maintain your motivation and commitment.

For example, if you want to complete your first triathlon but you've never run a mile in your life, you would be setting a goal that was beyond your current capabilities. If you decided instead to train for a five-mile race in six months, you would be setting an achievable goal.

4. Relevant

Relevant – or realistic – goals are goals that have a logical place in your life or your overall business strategy. The goal's action plan can be reasonably integrated into your life, with a realistic amount of effort.

For example, if your goal is to train to climb to base camp at Mount Everest within one year and you're about to launch a start-up business, you may need to question the relevance of your goal in the context of your current commitments.

5. Timely

It is essential for every goal to be attached to a time-frame – otherwise it is merely a dream. Check in to make sure that your time-frame is realistic - not too short, or too long. This will keep you motivated and committed to your action plan, and allow you track your progress.

Autosuggestion + Visualization

Autosuggestion and visualization are two techniques that can assist you in achieving your goals. Some of the most well-known and successful people in the world use these techniques, and it is no coincidence that they are masters in their own fields of business and sport. A few of these people include:

- Michael Phelps (Olympic Swimmer)
- Serena Williams (Tennis)
- Oprah Winfrey (Media Executive)
- Wayne Gretzky (Hockey)
- Bill Gates (Microsoft)
- Tyler Perry (Entertainment)

Of course, each of these people have a high degree of talent, ambition, intelligence and drive. However, to reach the top of their respective field, they have each used Autosuggestion and Visualization.

Autosuggestion

Autosuggestion is your internal dialogue; the constant stream of thoughts and comments that flows through your mind, and impacts what you think about yourself and how you perceive situations.

Since you were a small child, this self-talk has been influenced by your experiences and has programmed your mind to think and react in certain ways. The good news is that you can reprogram your mind and customize your self-talk any way you like. That is the power of Autosuggestion.

To begin practicing Autosuggestion, make sure you are relaxed and open to trying the technique; an ideal time is just before bed, or when you have some time to sit quietly. Then, repeat positive affirmations to yourself about the ideal outcome. Top sports and business people will often practice just before a big game or meeting.

Some examples of positive self-talk or autosuggestion include:

- I will lead my team to a victory tonight!
- I will be relaxed open to meeting new people at the party tonight!
- I will deliver a clear and impacting speech!
- I will stop worrying and tackle this problem tomorrow!
- I will stand up for my own ideas in the meeting!
- I will remember everything I have studied for the test tomorrow!

Visualization

Visualization is a practice complementary to Autosuggestion. While you can repeat affirmations to yourself over and over, combining this practice with visualization is twice as powerful.

Visualization is exactly what it sounds like: repeatedly visualizing how something is going to happen in your mind's eye. Nearly everyone in sports practices this technique. It has been proven to enhance performance better than practice alone.

This technique can easily be applied to business. For example, prior to any presentation or meeting where you must speak, present or "perform." You can also visualize yourself being incredibly productive and effective in your office. Or, having a discussion with your spouse calmly and rationally.

Elements to think about during visualization:

- What does the room look like?
- What do the people in the room look like?
- What is their mood? How do they receive me?
- What image do I project?
- How do I look?
- How do I behave? What is my attitude?
- What is the outcome?

6

Copywriting for Profits

When it comes to marketing, we all know that *what* you say is just as important as *how* you say it.

In fact, I would argue that how you say something is even more important than what you have to say.

Think about it. The whole purpose of communicating is to get a message to its intended audience. In business, this means telling your target market why they should buy your product or service, and why they should buy it from you.

You could have the best, most irresistible offer out there, but if you can't get your audience to pay attention to your ad, it's worthless. You may offer the solution to their biggest frustration, but if you can't get them to read beyond your headline, it means nothing.

Effective copywriting gets your message to your target audience and then leads them to act. **Effective copywriting gets you the sale.**

Good Copy, Bad Copy

There are several misconceptions out there when it comes to copywriting for marketing collateral.

The first is that good copy must be clever (or witty, funny, dramatic, ironic, etc.). People get wrapped up in the idea that their ads need to compete with the ads on the pages of Vanity Fair – or the New York Times. They feel that their campaign needs to be littered with clever words that allude to the pop culture of the day or position their company as "hip" or sophisticated.

This, in my experience, is rubbish.

The second assumption most business owners make is that good copy is the backbone of a successful ad or marketing campaign. I can't tell you how many good copywriters I've seen take the blame for a bad offer, or poorly positioned product.

The third misconception is that you need to be a good writer to write good copy. Or, if you're not a good writer, that you need to spend thousands of dollars on a copywriter for each of your marketing pieces.

That's rubbish, too.

So, then, what is good copy? And how do you write it?

The Purpose of Your Copy

Here are the key points you need to remember when crafting your advertisements:

a) A good headline *gets your readers to read the first sentence.*
b) A good first sentence *gets your readers to read the second sentence.*
c) And so on and on until the end of your marketing piece; or, the close of the sale.

Simple, isn't it?

The copy in your marketing materials is intended to persuade your audience to buy what you have to offer – one sentence at a time. Once you understand that copywriting is persuasive writing, not creative or technical writing, you will have much more success with your copywriting efforts.

Persuasive copy can be written in a number of ways – which we will discuss later in the section – but always includes:

- a compelling, shocking, or gripping headline
- a strong promise
- a heavy focus on benefits, not features
- proof to back up your claims

Compelling writing slowly builds a case and leads the reader down a specific path to the final destination – the sale. The argument or message is built up over several sentences, or paragraphs, until the reader is primed and ready for the question.

For example, if you came right out in your headline and said, "Buy Tommy's Sprockets to Solve Your Problems," your highly skeptical audience would not give your ad a second glance. You've asked for the sale right up front, before building some trust and slowly persuading your readers.

However, if you took the time to build your case, the ad would read something like this:

DON'T BUY ANOTHER SPROCKET UNTIL YOU READ THIS

Did you know that the average sprocket is made with only 25% authentic materials? To speed up production and reduce costs, sprocket manufacturing over the last decade has begun to rely heavily on artificial materials.

Would you trust the safety of your family to a product that reduces quality to preserve profit?

At Tommy's Sprockets, we put the safety of your family first. Our sprockets are stronger and safer, because we still make them the old-fashioned way – with 100% authentic materials and a lifetime guarantee.

Sure, they cost a little more than the average sprocket, but how much more would you pay for the safety of your family?

This ad isn't going to win any Pulitzer Prizes, but it doesn't need to. It engages the audience, communicates benefits, supports with features, and paints a compelling argument.

Headlines

Headlines are so crucial to the copywriting in your advertisement or sales letter that they deserve an entire section in this chapter.

Your headline is the first chance you have to make an impression on your target audience. Quite possibly, it is also your only chance. Without a headline that grabs your reader by the neck and focuses on what you have to say, the remainder of your ad is useless.

That's why even the greatest copywriters spend 50% of their time on the headline, and 50% on the rest of the copy.

With that in mind, it's important to note that your headline needs to do more than simply grab the attention of your potential readers. It also needs to tell them why they should care – your headline needs to send a full message that informs and encourages them to read onwards.

The most effective way to do this is to make an offer or promise to the reader that makes the time they invest in reading your ad worthwhile.

Seems like a lot for 8 to 10 words, doesn't it?

Headline Length

The general understanding when it comes to headline length is the shorter the better. But this comes from headline creation for newspapers and magazines, where space is crunched, and nothing is up for sale.

In fact, based on studies done in the direct mail industry, 40% to 50% of the most effective headlines are more than eight words in length – meaning there are really no hard and fast rules for headline length.

Another marketing example of headline length is in sales letters. I'm sure you've seen headlines in sales letters that actually comprise small paragraphs. This is the opposite way of thinking from newspaper headlines, but in this medium it works.

The point is, if you need more than eight words to get your message across, then use more.

Headline Readers: The 80/20 Rule

According to readership statistics, eight out of ten people read headlines, but only two of ten will read the rest of the advertisement or letter. This proves the importance of crafting powerful, meaningful headlines. It also proves that an effective headline is the golden key to getting the rest of the piece read.

So, it would stand to reason that the better your headline, the higher the chances of improving the averages in these statistics.

Headline Types

Direct Headlines simply state the offer or proposition in as clear a manner as possible. *All winter clothing 30% off.*

News Headlines typically announce a new product or piece of information and mimic a headline you would read in a newspaper. *Jonny launches new line of improved sprockets.*

The Question Headline asks a question that the reader can relate to or would be compelled to read on to find the answer. *Do you want clearer skin?*

The 'How to' Headline tells the reader the body copy or product will explain step by step instructions for something of interest to the reader. *How to save $1,000 in energy costs this year.*

Command Headline is one of the strongest headline types, and commands the reader to do something. *Make your dreams come true today.*

The '7 Reasons Why' Headline tells the reader the body copy will include 7 (or another number less than seven) points that will either back up a claim or illustrate product benefits. *7 reasons why your teenagers won't listen to you.*

Testimonial Headlines leverages the power of outsider and expert opinion and quotes them directly in the headline. *"Tommy's sprockets have changed my life" says Brad Pitt.*

In summary, your headline should:

- Be immediately engaging
- Be useful and relevant to the reader
- Convey information
- Trigger an emotional reaction
- Include an offer
- Intrigue your audience

Strategies for Better Copywriting

Simplify, Simplify, Simplify

Good copy is written in clear, simple language with short sentence structure. It's conversational and reads like you are speaking to a friend or colleague.

Important points – like benefits – are listed in numbered or bullet format and traditional grammar is sacrificed for brevity.

Always read your copy before you finalize it and take out any unnecessary words. Find the shortest way to communicate the most information.

Be More Persuasive

Persuasion is an important technique for structuring your copy. While there is no clear formula for any type of copywriting, persuasive copy consistently includes the following elements:

- Has a reader focus from the very beginning
- Each paragraph or section supports the main argument
- Is highly specific and provides proof to support claims
- Includes credible proof like statistics and expert opinion
- Returns the focus to the reader as often as possible

Persuasive writing convinces the reader that they should believe what you say and do what you say, and that there is something in it for them if they do. Again, there is no formula for this and no clear content rules, but there are some strategies you can use to make your writing more persuasive.

Repeat your point over and over

Repetition is a powerful and essential tool when crafting persuasive copy. It often will take several attempts at communicating before someone truly understands what you're saying. The benefit is that the more you say it, and the more ways you say it, the more likely your audience will believe it.

Of course, don't literally repeat yourself verbatim in your copy. Use a few different techniques to communicate the same point – for example, state it directly, tell a story, then repeat it again in your summary.

Give them reasons why

Backup your claims and requests with good reasons and leverage the power of the word 'because.' Studies have proven that even if the reason doesn't make any sense, or isn't directly related to the claim, people will be more likely to believe you simply based on the fact you backed up what you had to say.

Make comparisons to prove a point

Use the power of metaphors, analogies, and similes in your writing. This gives you an opportunity to relate the point you are trying to make directly to something the reader can relate to and understands to be true.

This is effective for making comparisons between like subjects, as well as unlike subjects, depending on the point you are trying to make.

Answer silent objections

Show that you understand the reader's point of view and thought process by answering questions you know they will be considering in their minds.

While you will not be able to address all potential objections in a single piece or think of all potential objections your reader may raise, you can definitely dispute the most common arguments against what you are claiming.

Tell a story

Storytelling is an effective technique to use in all aspects of your copywriting. People relate to the experiences of others and strive to learn from or compare themselves to the characters in the anecdotes. The story ends up doing the persuading for you.

Focus on Benefits

This is an obvious aspect of your messaging that you will feature in every piece you write, but it's not always easy to do well. Many writers end up featuring a slew of fake benefits instead of real ones.

Real benefits are things the reader cares about. For example, if you sold cough syrup you would want to explain how it eases the cold or flu symptoms, and not that it cures the illness. The symptoms are what are bothering the reader – that's what aspect of the product they care about and will make their purchase based on.

Make a Better Offer

Compel the reader to act with a stronger offer – one that they just can't possibly refuse. Make one that seems just believable enough to take action and reap the rewards.

A strong offer features a product or service with a high perceived value for a low cost. It could be a package of products offered for a lower price than the sum of the individual products, or a "free gift" with purchase.

Use Words that Work

Another misconception when it comes to copywriting is that it needs to be 100% unique. I'm not saying you should blatantly plagiarize other writer's work, but you should definitely pay attention to what works.

This includes how an ad is structured, how a point is made, or the hierarchy of the content. It also includes word choice. Certain words in marketing have been proven to have a stronger impact on general consumers than others.

There are tools that are easily available to you that will provide a list or database of effective words for use in advertising. Research online or invest in a software program like Glyphs to use as a resource.

Offer a Guarantee

A guarantee is another technique that will compel a potential customer to take action. A strong guarantee takes the risk involved in purchase decisions away from the customer and puts it on the seller.

Tell your customer that if your product or service doesn't deliver the performance or results you have promised, you'll give them their money back or compensate them in a way that will make it right.

7

How to Create Repeat Business and Have Clients that Pay, Stay and Refer

When it comes to marketing and generating more income, most business owners are focused outward.

They've carefully established and segmented their target market and created specific offers and messages for each market segment. They spend thousands of dollars in advertising and direct mail campaigns in hot pursuit of more leads, more customers, and more foot traffic.

While this is an effective way to build a business, it is costly and time consuming. It requires constant and consistent effort, and while this approach does generate results, those results quickly disappear when the effort stops or becomes less intense.

Successful businesses that see sustained growth have a double-edged marketing strategy. They focus their efforts *outward* – on new potential customers and marketing – as well as *inward* – on existing customers and referral business.

These successful businesses have leveraged their existing efforts to generate more revenue. Simply put, their customers buy from them repeatedly.

For most businesses, this is the easiest way to increase their revenues. Simple customer loyalty strategies and outstanding customer service are often all you need to dramatically increase your sales – from the customers you already have.

The Cost of Your Customers

Do you know how much it costs your business to buy new customers?

Each new customer that walks through your door – with the exception of referrals – has cost you money to acquire. You have spent money on advertising and promotions to generate leads and turn those leads into customers.

For example, if you have placed an ad in your local newspaper for $1,000, and the ad brings in 10 customers, you have paid $100 to acquire each customer. You would need to ensure each of those customers spent at least $200 to cover your margin and break even.

Alternately, if you spent two hours of your time and $10 per month on an email marketing program to send a newsletter to your existing database of customers, and you bring in 10 customers as a result – each customer has cost you $1.

Generating more repeat business means focusing on the marketing strategies that aim to keep your existing customers instead of purchasing new ones – effectively reducing the cost of attracting new customers to your business.

These strategies are simple to implement, and don't require much time investment. Just a solid understanding of how to make customers want to come back and spend more of their money

Keeping Your Customers

Marketing strategies that focus on keeping your current customer base are easy and enjoyable to implement. They allow you to build real relationships with the people you do business with, instead of dealing with a revolving door of people on the other end of your sales process.

Repeat customers create a community of people around your business that presumably share the same needs, desires and frustrations. The information you gain from these customers (market research) can help you strengthen your understanding of your target audience, and more accurately segment it.

Remember – 80% of your revenue comes from 20% of your customers. Always focus on these customers. They are ideal customers that you want to recruit and hold on to.

Customer Service: Make them love buying from you

Every business – even those with excellent service standards can improve the service they provide their customers. Customer service seems to be a dying concept in most businesses; more focus seems to be placed on the speed of the transaction. These days you can even go to the grocery store now and not speak to a single sales associate thanks to self-serve checkouts.

To improve your company's customer service standards, take a survey of your customers and your employees to brainstorm ways you can improve the experience of buying from your business.

Successful customer service standards – those that make your customers *buy* – are:

Consistent. The standards are kept up by every person in your organization. Expectations are clear and followed through. Customers know what to expect and choose your business because of those expectations.

Convenient. It is nearly effortless for the customer to spend money at your place of business. Convenience can take many forms – location, product selection, value-added services like delivery – and it is also consistent.

Customer-driven. The service the customer receives is exactly how they would like to be treated when buying your product or service. It is reflective of your target market, and appropriate to their lifestyle. Customers would probably not appreciate white linen tablecloths at a fast food restaurant, but they would appreciate a 2-minutes or less guarantee.

Newsletters: Keep in touch with your customers

A regular newsletter is an easy, time-effective, and inexpensive marketing strategy to implement. Unfortunately, many small businesses think these are too time consuming and too expensive to adopt as part of their marketing strategy.

The most popular type of newsletter distribution is email. This will cost your business as little at $10 per month for an email marketing service subscription and can be customized to your unique branding.

Here is an easy five-step process to starting a company newsletter:

1. **Pick your audience.** New customers? Market segment? Existing customers?
2. **Choose what you're going to say.** Company news? Feature product? New offer?
3. **Determine how you're going to say it.** Articles? Bullet points? Pictures?
4. **Decide how it's going to get to your audience.** Email? Mail? In-store?
5. **Track your results.** How many people opened it? Read it? Took action?

Value Added Service: Give them happy surprises

Adding value to your business is an effective way of getting your customers back. Every person I know would choose a mattress store that offered free delivery over one that did not. It's that simple.

There are many ways to add value to your business, including:

- **Feature your expertise.** Use your knowledge to provide additional value to your customers. Offer a free consumer guide or report with every purchase.

- **Add convenience services.** Offer a service that makes their purchase easier, or more convenient. The best example of this is free shipping or delivery.

- **Package complementary services**. Packaging like items together creates an increase in perceived value. This is great for start-up kits.

- **Offer new products or services**. Feature top of the line or exclusive products, available only at your business. Offer a new service or profile a new staff member with niche expertise.

Value added services generate repeat customers in one of two ways:

1. Impress them on their first visit. Impress you customer with great service, a product that meets their needs, and then wow them with something extra that they weren't expecting. Get them to associate the experience of dealing with your business with happy surprises and create a perception of higher value.

2. Entice them to come back. The introduction of a new value-added service can be enough to convince a customer to buy from you again. Their initial purchase established a trust and knowledge of your business and its processes. They will want to "be included" in anything new you have to offer – especially if there is exclusivity. It is easier to attract clients that have purchased from you than potential clients who have not.

Customer Loyalty Programs: Give them incentives

Another simple way to keep in touch with existing customers and keep them coming back to you is to create a customer loyalty program.

These programs do not have to be complicated or costly and are relatively easy to maintain once they have been implemented. These programs help you gain more information on your customers and their purchasing habits.

Here are some examples of simple loyalty programs that you can implement:

Free product or service. Give them every 10th (or 6th) product or service free. Produce stamp cards with your logo and contact information on it.

Reward dollars. Give them a certain percentage of their purchase back in money that can only be spent in-store. Produce "funny money" with your logo and brand.

Rewards points. Give them a certain number of points for every dollar they spend. These points can be spent in-store, or on special items you bring in for points only.

Membership amenities. Give members access to VIP amenities that are not available to other customers. Produce member cards or give out member numbers.

Remember that in order for this strategy to work, you and your team have to understand and promote it. The program in itself becomes a product that you sell.

8

How to Profit through Time Management

Manage Time Like Money

Why did you get into business for yourself? Was it to be your own boss? Choose your own hours? Have more time with the family? Spend more time doing what you love? Chances are, you answered yes to all these questions.

These days, you probably wonder where the time went. Why you spent 12 hours at work and barely make a dent in your to-do list. We already know that time is a key resource for you and your business, but it's also a key resource in your life. Harnessing and leveraging time is the only way to enjoy life and have a profitable business at the same time.

Most business owners carefully manage their financial and personnel resources, and pay close attention to their performance. Marketing plans and budgets are created, people are hired and fired. What most business owners don't realize is that time – and the time of all employees – requires the same attention and diligent management.

Time will never manage itself. The decision to make a pro-active effort to manage your time must come from you. Once you have committed to taking ownership for your own time management, there are a host of tools available to you. But first, you must understand how much your time is worth, and where you are currently spending it.

What is Your Time Worth?

Ever wonder what your time is actually worth? Here's a quick way to figure it out:

Target annual income	A.
Working days in a year	B. 235
Working hours in a day	C. 7
Working hours in a year	D. 1,645
A ÷ D = YOUR HOURLY WORTH (before tax + expenses)	E.

This is a very simple calculation intended to put your time in perspective. In reality, no one is productive for each of the 1,645 hours. Various studies have put actual productivity at anywhere between 25 minutes and four hours per day. Either way, there's a lot of room for improvement.

Let's look at it another way:

Your age	A.
Days in a year	B.
Days spent on earth to date (A x B)	C.
Average life expectancy	D. 70
Total projected days on earth (D x B)	E.

Estimated days left (E – C)	F.

This exercise isn't intended to scare you but bring your attention to the importance of choosing how you spend each hour you have available. It is a choice! By developing the skills required to manage your time, you will not only have a profitable business, but a rewarding and balanced life.

The Five Culprits of Time Theft

Chances are – if you're like most people – you have no idea where your time goes. You're likely frustrated by the fact that you can spend 10, 12, even 14 hours a day working, and not make a dent in your to-do list, or only bill half of those hours.

When we're too busy and overloaded with work, we often switch into reactive mode. We can't make it to the bottom of the pile and end up handling issues and making decisions at the last minute. One of the great benefits of choosing to become proactive in time management is that you can become proactive in all other areas of your business. When in proactive mode, you can take steps to grow your business through networking, building programs, and establishing systems.

Before you investigate where your time goes, let's look at the top five culprits of modern-day time theft:

1. Your Email

How many times a day do you check your email? Is Outlook or Mail constantly running on your desktop? Email – internal, external, personal and business – clogs up your day like no other communication channel. For many of us, it is possible to spend the entire day writing and responding to emails without even glancing at our inbox. The number of emails sent and received each day by the average person in 2017 was 161. Multiply that by an average of two minutes per message, and you have spent over five hours on email in a single day.

2. Your Cell Phone (Or Blackberry)

Cell phones have created convenience, security, and the luxury of telecommuting – but they don't call it a Blackberry for nothing. PDAs and cell phones have also created a society that expects to be able to reach you at any moment, or at least receive instant responses to their calls. Your cell phone or PDA not only robs you of your time during the day, but also during the evenings and on weekends when you are not at work.

3. Your Open-Door Policy

If you make it easy for your staff and associates to interrupt you, they will. Too often, open-door policies are set up by human resource departments to create clear communication channels. Instead, they create a clog of employees lined up at your door seeking immediate answers to non-emergent issues.

4. Meetings

How many times have you been to a meeting that was scheduled to be an hour, and ended up lasting three? How often do you attend unnecessary meetings? Or meetings that run off-topic? Meetings can be a huge source of wasted time – your valuable time. In a senior management or ownership position, your day may consist of back-to-back meetings, leaving only your evening hours to complete the tasks that should have been done during the day.

5. YOU!

Every person has daily habits that sabotage their ability to work productively and efficiently. Many entrepreneurs and business owners can't separate business hours from leisure hours. Some get caught in a time warp while surfing the internet. Others - mainly overachievers – can become paralyzed by perfectionism or procrastination. Mainly we just don't have the tools to schedule and structure our time in a way that fits with our working style.

Where Does Your Time Go?

So far, we've seen that time is a resource that should be as carefully managed as cash, we've figured out what your time is worth, and looked at the top five culprits of time theft. You've committed to taking steps to become a better time manager. What now?

Personal Time Management Research Exercise

The next step is to take a good, (and honest!) look at how you spend your time. Once you understand your patterns and habits, you begin to implement the strategies in this chapter that will make you a better time manager.

Step One: Time Audit

Use the Time Log Worksheet at the back of this chapter to record how you spend your time for three working days in a row. Be honest and be specific. Include time spent in transit, surfing the web, interacting with clients and colleagues, as well as how your time is spent at home in the evenings. The more information you can record, the easier it will be to analyze your time management skills in step two.

Step Two: Time Categorization

Once you have recorded your time for three days, sit down with all three sheets in front of you and identify the following using different colored markers or highlighters:

- Driving, public transportation or other travel
- Eating, including food preparation
- Personal Errands
- Exercise
- Watching TV
- Sleeping, including naps
- Using the computer, personal use only
- Being with family / friends
- Emailing, including checking, reading, and returning messages

- Talking on the phone, including checking and returning messages
- Internal meetings
- External meetings
- Administrative work
- Client work
- Non-client, non-administrative work

Step Three: Time Analysis

Now that you have identified how you have spent your time, go through the worksheets one more time and identify if you have spent enough, too much, or too little time on each main task.

Then, based on your observations, answer the following questions:

1. What patterns do you notice about how you spend your time during the day? (i.e., When are you most productive? Least productive? Most or least interrupted?)

_____

_____

_____

_____

_____

_____

2. Write down the four highest priorities in your life right now. Does your timesheet reflect these priorities?

_____

_____

_____

_____

_____

3. If you have more time, what would you do?

_____

_____

_____

_____

4. If you had less time, what wouldn't you do?

_____

_____

_____

5. Could you remove the items in question four and add the items in question three? Why or why not?

_____

_____

_____

_____

6. Is procrastination a problem for you? How much?

_____

_____

_____

_____

Strategies for Profitable Time Management

There are many ways to curb time theft and refine your time management ability. Through a solid understanding of how you currently spend – and waste – time, you can determine which strategies you need to implement to correct unproductive behavior.

Here are 17 ways you can turn **less** of your time into **more** money:

1. Set Clear Priorities

The foundation of time management a clear understanding of what your time is best spent on. Once you accept that you can't do everything, you need to decide what needs to be completed now, what can be completed later, and what someone else can complete. Each to-do list you create should be put through this filter and reorganized so the highest priority items are on top, and the lowest priority items are less visible, or on the bottom.

Once you have established your priorities – which will also naturally reflect the priorities and goals of your business – stick to them. Just because someone else feels something is of a high priority doesn't mean it holds the same status next to your other tasks.

Prioritization is also helpful in your personal life and leisure time. Your spare time is precious – so make sure you are clear on how you would like to spend it.

2. Use Your Skills – Delegate Your Weaknesses

As a business owner, your day naturally consists of tasks you dislike doing. Some are essential – signing checks, reviewing financial statements, and other business maintenance – while others are simply not within your skill set.

If you are a strong public speaker, but struggle with report writing – delegate to a copywriter or editor. If you own a retail store and have no experience in design – outsource your signage. These freelance professionals often cost half as much as you and take half as long to complete the task. Your time is saved for tasks that use and strengthen your skills effectively, your stress is managed, and ultimately a better product is produced.

3. Delegate, Delegate, Delegate

As a small business owner, the only way you will ever get everything done is by delegating. Delegation is a vital skill that needs to be refined and practiced, and once mastered is the key to profitable time management.

Too often, owners and managers believe that it will be "faster" or "more efficient" to complete the task themselves than to train and monitor someone else. Other times, there are no internal resources to download assignments to.

As a result, the following trends can be seen in many small companies:

- Owners and senior staff are stressed and overworked, while junior staff are underutilized and under capacity.

- Staff members are not given an opportunity to grow and develop in their roles and may perceive a lack of trust or confidence in their ability. The company loses good people.

- Owners and senior staff are always in a reactive state, instead of a visionary or proactive state.

- Delegation happens at the very last minute, and junior staff has little understanding of either the overall project or expectations for the task.

The easiest way to fix this problem is before it starts. Create a solid team of staff members around you who are well-trained and prepared to support the business. Attract and retain qualified and quality people who can be cross-trained and promoted within the company. Ensure that communication flows throughout the business, so everyone has the product and service knowledge to step in and assist when necessary.

4. Learn to Say "No"

It's easy to fall into the habit of saying yes to everything. You are, after all the business owner, right? No one can complete these tasks as well as you, right? You'll lose that customer if you don't help them with their garage sale, right?

Wrong. The most successful business owners have a keen understanding of how their time is best spent, and *delegate* the remaining responsibilities to trusted others. It's too easy to say yes to every request in the moment, and later feel overwhelmed when it's added to your to do list. You may not ruffle any feathers, but what toll does it take on your stress level? Your workload? Your time is valuable – so protect it!

Remember that if it is too challenging to say no immediately, you can always request some time to think about it. This way, you can evaluate your workload and realistically decide whether you can take on a new project. Then, stand by your decision, or assist in bringing in the necessary resources to get it done.

5. Create (and keep!) a Strict Schedule

While multi-tasking is a desirable skill, it is also often a time thief. Attempting to do too many things at one time ensures that nothing gets done. As a business owner, you need to be able to focus and concentrate on essential projects without interruptions.

The only way to do this is the commit to a strict schedule. Once you understand your work style and concentration patterns, you can allocate periods of the day to specific tasks. This includes personal and leisure time – schedule it and stick to it.

Schedule time for: list-creation + prioritization, email messages, telephone messages, internal meetings, client meetings, meeting preparation, "me-time," family time, recreation + fitness, daily business tasks, and blocks for focused work.

Remember that there is a training period involved in beginning a new routine – for yourself and those around you. Use your voicemail, out-of-office email message, and a closed door to begin to let people know when you will not be disturbed.

6. Make Decisions

The choice to not make a decision is a decision in itself. The most successful business owners have the ability to make good decisions quickly and efficiently, and do not waste time deliberating over simple choices.

In leadership positions, often people are afraid of making the wrong decision or looking foolish if they make a mistake in front of junior staff. What they don't realize, is that hesitating or avoiding decision making impacts their leadership just as much or more than making the wrong decision. Not only can being indecisive be personally stressful, but it is also stressful for those around you whose tasks are waiting on your choices.

Remember, you must make the best decision with the information you have, in the time frame you have to make the decision. No one expects you to be a fortune teller – be decisive, make some mistakes, and learn from them.

7. Manage Telephone Interruptions

This is a huge source of time theft that can easily be managed and avoided. If you are available to take phone calls at any time of day, you are setting yourself up to take work home in the evenings. The phone will always ring when you are focused on an important task, and this is something can easily be avoided.

Figure out when you are most productive. Is it in the morning or the afternoon? Before, during, or after lunch? Once you have identified this time period, set your phone on "do not disturb" or have your calls directed to voicemail. If you do not have a receptionist, a variety of automatic answering systems are available for a nominal fee. To structure your phone time further, let callers know on your voicemail what specific time of day is best to reach you via phone. Then, set that time aside to receive and return phone calls.

8. Keep Your Work Environment Organized

Have you ever tried to make dinner in a messy kitchen? More of your time is spent looking for (and cleaning) dishes and tools than spent cooking the meal.

The same goes for your work environment. If your desk and office is in a constant state of chaos, then your mind will be too. In fact, some studies have revealed that the average senior business leader spends nearly four weeks each year navigating through messy or cluttered desks, looking for lost information. Does that sound like productive time to you?

Once you make the initial clean sweep, it's easy to maintain order in the chaos:

- Tidy your desk at the beginning and end of each day. Attach pertinent documents to your to do list or have clear and organized folders for loose papers.

- Organize your supplies drawer so you have easy access to stationery like pens, post-it notes, staplers and highlighters. Every minute counts!

- Only have the documents and files you are working on, on your desk. The rest should be neatly filed on a side table for later retrieval.

- Keep personal items (like photos or memorabilia) out of your primary line of vision. These can be distracting and encourage daydreaming.

As for your office or store, there are many ways to make its layout more conducive to effective time management. Try:

- Minimizing the distance between the reception desk and electronics like photocopies and fax machines.

- Keep a clear line of sight between your office and the most productive area of your business, so you are aware of what is happening amongst your staff.

- Organize shelves and filling cabinets so files are not only easily accessed, but out of sight when not being used. Consider putting sliding doors or cabinets in storage areas and remember that the floor is not a storage cabinet.

9. Keep Your Filing System Organized

If your data isn't organized properly, you will waste hundreds of hours searching for documents you need on a regular basis. This includes both electronic and hard copy files; they need to be organized and up to date.

Customer databases and enquiry records are worth their weight in gold. You can't afford to get behind when updating this information, or poorly store it for later retrieval. There are many easy to use software programs that will manage and organize customer databases for you; it doesn't need to be a time consuming or tedious exercise.

A simple way to manage information is to keep it in short, medium, and long-term files for both hard and electronic copies. Create shortcuts on your desktop for folders or files you constantly access. Have short-term files available on your desk, medium-term files available within an arm's reach, and long-term files stored in cabinets.

10. Clearly Communicate – Never Assume

One of the biggest issues for time management in business – and likely the world – is miscommunication. This is a dangerous issue that can cripple any business, including yours. Establishing and enforcing clear policies on things like accurate note taking, task assignments, and phone messages will ensure your staff understand the importance of clear and accurate communication.

The easiest habit to start to curb miscommunication is simple: write everything down. Carry a notepad, and jot down key points, figures, agreements and deadlines. Don't assume you'll remember later – you have at least a hundred other things to remember.

Some other simple strategies are:

- Return all communication promptly, including email, letters, faxes and phone calls

- Repeat back phone messages, phone numbers and other figures to confirm you recorded the information correctly.

- Record appointments in your PDA or agenda the moment you make them. Otherwise, you will forget.

- Double check and confirm everything – addresses, phone numbers, meeting locations and times.

- Maintain accurate customer contact logs with dates, times, and phone numbers.

- Post checklists in your store or office for routine operations procedures.

- Announce any changes to the policies and procedures manual immediately.

11. Stop Duplicating Efforts

This is a key element of time management that is closely related to effective communication. Studies have continually shown that many businesses often duplicate and triplicate efforts that need only be completed once.

When you have clear systems and procedures in place, your staff will not need to "reinvent the wheel" each time the task needs to be completed. Meeting minutes and individual task assignments will ensure everyone is on the same page and understands their personal responsibilities.

Simple examples of this include re-reading your to-do list each hour to determine what the next important item is. If your list is already structured by priority, this is a needless task. If two staff members are working on similar projects, but unaware of the other, the work will not only be inconsistent, but the efforts will be duplicated. These are easy problems to fix, once they have been identified and communicated.

12. Say Goodbye to Procrastination + Perfectionism

Procrastination is something we all face at one time or another – and likely have since our school days. However, given the pace that the world operates at today, you will only fall behind your competitor if you allow procrastination to rule your day. So how you do avoid it? It's simple. Stop, and just get started, no matter how boring, tedious, or painful the project may be. Reward yourself by crossing each step off your to-do list.

Many small business owners also fall victim to perfectionism, which can be paralyzing. The fear that there isn't enough time or resources to "get it perfect" will sometimes stop you dead in your tracks. Perfectionism can also hinder your ability to delegate and say no to tasks you believe no one else can complete "better". Do the best you can with the time and resources you have – and just get started.

13. Plan Your Work, Work Your Plan

Have you ever placed an advertisement on the fly because it was "cheaper," "faster," or "more urgent" than creating a marketing plan? Do you and your staff have a clear idea of where your business is headed over the next 6 to 12 months, or 5 years?

Many studies show that less than 10% of small businesses have up to date marketing and business plans, as compared to the majority of large corporations and public companies, which have both.

Marketing and business plans take time and effort to create – but they work and pay off in spades. They also save you time and money as compared to a haphazard or fly-by-the-seat-of-your-pants strategy. With a marketing plan in place, you will have an idea of how many ads you will be placing in a year, which will earn you a volume discount. Your marketing materials will complement each other and deliver the same message to the same target audience. Designers will charge less for a package of collateral than for individual collateral items.

A business plan will provide you with a guide to reference when making decisions. You can repeatedly ask if the endeavor at hand will contribute to your overall vision, or just seems like a good idea or price.

Remember that planning includes both short and long-term time frames, and applies to both your daily to-do list, and your marketing budget. It provides you with a means to measure your progress, assists in identifying priorities, and helps to manage your time.

14. Avoid Needless, Impromptu + Unstructured Meetings

This may seem like a time theft issue that is out of your control, but it's not. You are in control of your own time, and through strict scheduling can establish a structure for internal and external meetings that everyone around you can work within.

Minimize impromptu internal meetings by letting your staff know when you're available for a "quick chat" and when you are not. If it is important, ask them to schedule a time to meet with you that works with both of your schedules. This not only saves you time but encourages staff to find solutions to their own issues, and only approach you with more urgent or challenging matters.

You can't avoid having meetings, but you can avoid having unstructured meetings. Ask for or create an agenda for each meeting you attend, with a clear objective and an amount of time allocated to each item. This will keep your meetings focused and on task. If a meeting does run late, give yourself a reasonable buffer, and politely leave for your next appointment. You can always follow up with a colleague to catch-up on the pertinent items you may have missed.

15. Establish Clear Policies + Procedures

A clear policy and procedures manual are like a marketing or business plan – it takes time to create, but ultimately saves everyone in your company time, money and effort. A step-by-step guide to "the way we do things here" is an invaluable resource for your existing and new staff, and provides clear expectations for how you like things done.

Too many businesses make up policies and procedures on the fly – creating dangerous scenarios where mistakes are made, and expectations are not clear. Some items that should be included in a comprehensive policy and procedures manual include:

- Recruitment
- Customer relations
- Customer enquiries
- Customer complaints
- Returns
- Exchanges

- Late Payments
- Salary structure
- Bonus structure
- Employee review
- Theft
- Harassment

16. Keep the Right Set of Tools

The equipment your business needs to operate (and grow!) effectively should always be on hand, or easily contracted out. This is specific to each company, and closely related to costs – including the cost of your time.

Whether you are a high-tech business or local retailer, knowledge of the latest advancements in technology will increase your efficiency. It will help you stay on top of the competitor, maintain your position as an expert, and perhaps provide an easier way of getting things done.

Always ask yourself if these purchases are essential to your business –could perhaps make these purchases from a second-hand dealer to minimize cost? Is it more cost effective to outsource or sub-contract the tasks to someone with access to this equipment, or to buy the equipment yourself?

If your business relies on tools and technology for daily tasks (such as the trades profession) then obtaining the best quality you can afford is crucial.

17. Maintain Your Equipment

This may seem obvious, but you'll understand the importance if your network server has ever crashed or point of sale system has malfunctioned. Your business can be slowed to a stand-still if your equipment is not in good working order. Of course there are instances that can't be predicted, but regular maintenance of your essential equipment will reduce these occurrences and help to anticipate when old equipment needs to be repaired or replaced.

Personal Time Management Strategy

Choose the top five tips from this chapter that you think will help you the most, given your personal time management research. Write them below, with three corresponding actions that you will start tomorrow. For example, if you are going to set a strict schedule, three actions might be to establish the schedule, communicate it to your staff, and re-record your voicemail message.

1. _____

    a. _____

    b. _____

    c. _____

2. _____

    a. _____

    b. _____

    c. _____

3. _____

    a. _____

    b. _____

    c. _____

4. _____

    a. _____

    b. _____

    c. _____

5. _____

    a. _____

    b. _____

    c. _____

Timesheet | Day One

Timeslot	Activities	More/Less/ Enough time?
7:00 – 7:30		
7:30 – 8:00		
8:00 – 8:30		
8:30 – 9:00		
9:00 – 9:30		
10:00 – 10:30		
10:30 – 11:00		
11:00 – 11:30		
11:30 – 12:00		
12:00 – 12:30		
12:30 – 1:00		
1:00 – 1:30		
1:30 – 2:00		
2:00 – 2:30		
2:30 – 3:00		
3:00 – 3:30		
3:30 – 4:00		
4:00 – 4:30		
4:30 – 5:00		
5:00 – 5:30		
5:30 – 6:00		
6:00 – 10:00 (Evening)		

Timesheet | Day Two

Timeslot	Activities	More/Less/ Enough time?
7:00 – 7:30		
7:30 – 8:00		
8:00 – 8:30		
8:30 – 9:00		
9:00 – 9:30		
10:00 – 10:30		
10:30 – 11:00		
11:00 – 11:30		
11:30 – 12:00		
12:00 – 12:30		
12:30 – 1:00		
1:00 – 1:30		
1:30 – 2:00		
2:00 – 2:30		
2:30 – 3:00		
3:00 – 3:30		
3:30 – 4:00		
4:00 – 4:30		
4:30 – 5:00		
5:00 – 5:30		
5:30 – 6:00		
6:00 – 10:00 (Evening)		

Timesheet | Day Three

Timeslot	Activities	More/Less/ Enough time?
7:00 – 7:30		
7:30 – 8:00		
8:00 – 8:30		
8:30 – 9:00		
9:00 – 9:30		
10:00 – 10:30		
10:30 – 11:00		
11:00 – 11:30		
11:30 – 12:00		
12:00 – 12:30		
12:30 – 1:00		
1:00 – 1:30		
1:30 – 2:00		
2:00 – 2:30		
2:30 – 3:00		
3:00 – 3:30		
3:30 – 4:00		
4:00 – 4:30		
4:30 – 5:00		
5:00 – 5:30		
5:30 – 6:00		
6:00 – 10:00 (Evening)		

Daily To-Do List | Business

Task	Priority (1-10)	Deadline?	Delegation?

Weekly To-Do List | Personal (Family, Leisure, etc.)

Task	Priority (1-10)	Deadline?	Delegation?

9

Risk Reversal to Increase Sales

What is the biggest objection you need to overcome when closing a sale? Is it cost? Belief in what you have to say? Confidence in your product or service?

While it is a different answer for every business, every business must deal with some element of customer fear or hesitation before a monetary transaction.

The reality is that even if you overcome these objections and close the sale, your customer walks away carrying 99% of the risk associated with the purchase. If the product doesn't work, breaks down, or doesn't perform to expectations, your customer has parted with their dollars in exchange for disappointment.

In marketing, your objective is to generate as many leads as possible, then to convert each lead into a customer, or sale. The ratio of leads to closed sales is called your conversion rate.

What if you could eliminate the risk involved in a transaction? Would you turn more leads into customers? The answer is absolutely.

Introducing a risk reversal element into your marketing message or unique offer is a powerful way to give yourself an edge on the competition and close more sales. But how exactly are you going to do this?

It's easy – just give them a guarantee.

The Power of Guarantees

What is Risk Reversal?

Risk reversal simply refers to reversing the risk associated with a transaction – transferring it from the customer to the vendor.

Everyone can think of a handful of times they have purchased a product or service that did not deliver on their expectations. A time where a salesperson made them a promise and did not deliver. A time where they *lost money* on a faulty product or bogus service.

Fear of being burned or taken advantage of prevents many people from spending their money. Customers can also be very wary of buying a product or service for the first time.

Providing a strong guarantee eliminates most of the risk involved in the purchase and breaks down natural barriers in the sales process. Guarantees will often shorten the sales process all together – skipping any discussion of objections – because the customer does not see any risk in "trying the product out."

There is also a growing consumer expectation when it comes to guarantees. Many stores will take back anything the customer has not been happy with and return money or store credit. Popular health food stores encourage customers to try new or unfamiliar products by promising a hassle-free, no questions asked return process. A guarantee or easy return policy can be the difference between choosing one business over its competition.

Your customers buy results, not products or services

The strongest guarantee you can make is on *results*, not products or services.

If you guarantee that your customer will receive the benefits or results, they are looking for, the specific product or service they'll need to achieve those results becomes irrelevant.

People buy benefits and results. For example, they don't buy water purifiers; they buy the benefit enjoying clean, fresh-tasting water. They don't buy lawn sprinkler systems; they buy a healthy green lawn.

Once you understand what specific benefit or solution your customers are seeking, find a way to guarantee they'll receive or experience that solution. If they don't, you'll compensate them for it.

Remember what you have guaranteed

While guarantees will increase sales for most businesses, they can also be the fast track to business failure if their product or service isn't a quality one. Take the time to ensure you have a strong offering before you implement a guarantee.

Guarantees are most effective when you are selling someone something they need or want – not when you are trying to convince someone to purchase something, they have no use for.

Increasing Conversion Rates with a Guarantee

Guarantees can help your business turn more qualified leads into repeat customers. Strong guarantees are big and bold, but also realistic. They're just a little bit better than your competition, but consistent with the industry's standards.

Your conversion rate

Your conversion rate is the percentage of clients you convert from leads into customers. The higher your conversion rate, the more revenue you will generate.

To figure out your conversion rate, divide the number of people who purchase from you by the number of people who inquired about your product or service. This will generate a percentage value of your conversion rate.

Guarantees encourage and increase conversion. They motivate potential customers to buy – and to buy from you – because you stand behind what you sell in a big way. There is no risk involved in purchasing what you have to offer.

Creating your guarantee

So, you're convinced your business – and your customers – would benefit from a strong guarantee. Now what? What are you going to guarantee? How are you going to position it?

Once again, this goes back to your target audience and your product or service. What are some of the major objections your potential customers raise during the sales process? What kind of risk do they take on when they make a purchase? How much time will they need to test or experience your product or service?

Brainstorm a list of things about your industry that really frustrate your customers. They could be service-based (contractors that don't show up, employees who don't perform) or product-based (products that break, do not perform). Then, look at your list and decide how you can make sure these things do not happen. Think big – you can do a lot more than you think – then determine if you can make good on your promise. If you can't guarantee the first frustration, then move on to the second.

Here are some tips on writing your guarantee:

- **Be specific.** Explain exactly what you are guaranteeing. Don't make vague guarantees that a product will "work" or a service will make you "happy". These words mean different things to different people. Guarantee specific performance or results.

- **Include a clear timeframe.** Put a realistic timeframe on your guarantee. Very few products or services are good forever. Offer a 30-day or 90-day free trial; guarantee results within a set number of days or weeks. This can protect your company and sets clear expectations for your clients.

- **Be bold.** Unbelievable guarantees get a customer's attention, so go as far as you realistically can with your claim. Find a way to stand out over the competition – which may also have a guarantee.

- **Tell them what you'll do.** Explain what you'll do – how you'll compensate them – if your product or service doesn't deliver. Be specific, talk money, and go above and beyond.

Implementing guarantees

Tell your clients!

Put your guarantee everywhere – your website, brochures, receipt tape, in-store signage, advertisements, and other promotional materials. It will only help attract customers if they know about it.

Send a newsletter to your existing client base informing them of your new guarantees – you never know how many customers you can convince to come back and spend more in your business.

Train your Staff

Once you have decided to offer your clients a guarantee, you need to ensure your staff are properly trained on the specific policies and procedures associated with that guarantee. If you offer different guarantees for different products and services, ensure this is made clear as well.

Presumably, your staff will be communicating the details of your guarantee, and fielding customer questions. They will have to know how to sell the product using the guarantee as a benefit and understand every application of the guarantee in your business. Every scenario a customer may need to use it.

To ensure your staff is not making any false claims or promises, create a guarantee script for them to use and stick to. This will prevent customers from returning with false hopes for their money back, or other compensation.

Returns + Claims

So, by now you must be thinking, "Great, I can convert more customers with a strong guarantee, and increase my sales. But what about the added risk I have taken on from my customers? Won't I start to see a ton of returns and service claims?" This is a valid question. Making a strong guarantee means standing by it and delivering on your promise. Inevitably, when you guarantee something, someone is going to take you up on that guarantee and make a claim. I'm going to answer this question in two parts:

1. Stand behind your product or service. You're not in business to scam customers. If you sell a product or service, and you believe in it enough to offer it to your customers, it is likely a quality product or genuine service.

If this is a concern to you, consider implementing strong quality controls or stronger criteria for your merchandising. Companies that offer products and services that deliver results can offer the strongest guarantees.

Of course, you will get returns. You will have customers come in to take advantage of you. Just remember that as long as the increase in sales outweighs the claims, your guarantee strategy has been successful.

2. Understand your customer's likely behavior. The truth is that most customers will never take advantage of your guarantee – regardless of their satisfaction level. There are several reasons for this.

The first is that most people can't be bothered to drive, mail, or otherwise seek a refund on an item under $50. Many let the timeframe slip by and have an "oh well" attitude.

The second is that most people don't like confrontation. There is usually an element of confrontation involved in telling someone you didn't like a product or service, and many people do not have the confidence to do so. They'd rather eat the cost than go through the process of asking for a refund.

Handling claims and returns:

If you do have your product returned, it is in your company's best interest to create a system for handling these customer interactions.

Create a claim form

Ensure that each customer who makes a claim about your product or service fills out a standard form. Doing so will help you prevent fraud, gather important information about the customer and their reasoning, and create a "hoop" for the customer to jump through if they want their money back.

Name
Date
Contact Information
Salesperson
Product
Reason for claim:
Comments
Follow-up

Keep a claim or return log

Create a log or filing system for your claims. This will give you a snapshot of your guarantee program, a record-keeping system, and a wealth of information about each customer's experience and motivations.

Use the information

Take the claim forms your customers have filled out and review them regularly. While some of the claims won't be genuine, there will be some real feedback you can use to improve your product or service, or to modify your guarantee. You may need to make it more realistic or change the specifics.

10

How to Create Newsletters for Your Business, Easily and Quickly

It's no secret that newsletters are a great way to maintain contact with your customer base, and to communicate offers, news, ideas, and expertise to potential clients. But how many email newsletters do you receive each week? Each day? And of those emails, how many do you open? How many do you read? I bet it's only a small fraction of those that land in your inbox.

The work involved with writing, producing, and distributing a newsletter for your business can be a time-consuming task. This is especially true when you are faced with having to compete with all the other information that your customers are bombarded with daily.

However, a regular company newsletter can be an important part of your marketing strategy, allowing you to build a stronger relationship with your clients and increase customer retention and the strength of your business.

So, what is the difference between newsletters that get opened, and ones that get junked? How do you make sure that the time and money you invest in this communication tool provides a measurable return?

Why Send Newsletters?

- **To build trust**. Newsletters are an effective way to forge stronger, trust-based relationships with your customers. They are an informal, newsy type of communication that can be highly personalized for individual recipients.

- **To update your customers**. Newsletters let your customers know about changes and developments in your business, including the comings of new employees and products or services.

- **To promote your products or services.** A strong newsletter will repeatedly reinforce your marketing message and keep your offering at the top of your customer's minds.

- **To stay in touch (and top of mind!).** Newsletters help you show your customers that they're important to your business, and that you haven't forgotten about them since they left your store.

- **To build a community around your business**. Regular newsletters that feature useful information and community events create a community of people with a common interest: your knowledge, expertise, and offering.

Writing an Effective Newsletter

An effective newsletter should be easy to read, contain interesting and relevant information, and be visually engaging. When you send information to your customer's inbox, you are asking them to invest their time in reading what you have to say. Make sure they finish feeling that their time was well spent.

Know who you are talking to. As with every other piece of marketing collateral, you must establish who you are trying to reach before you put your content together. Don't make the mistake of assuming everyone will be interested in what you have to say. Who are your readers? Are they internal (employees) or external (customers) to your organization? What are their interests? Do they like to be entertained or do they just want information? How much time do they have to read your newsletters?

Use language that they can easily read and understand. Are you talking to computer programmers or teenagers? Would you spend time reading a book that wasn't interesting or was written in a language you didn't understand? Speak to the readers using language and references that they will relate to.

Here are some helpful tips to consider when writing for your audience:

- Keep the tone informal and conversational
- Write in first person to establish a relationship

- Be direct – use as few words as possible and keep it simple
- Avoid flowery or overly descriptive language
- Stay away from salesy or advertising language

Provide Relevant and Interesting Content. The backbone of your newsletter is the content. Without solid, valuable content, even the most attractive and well-formatted newsletters are virtually ineffective.

With so many other things competing for your customer's attention, it is crucial to make your newsletter interesting and relevant. How does it add value to their lives? Why does it deserve their attention?

Keep it purpose-focused. Like every other piece of your marketing collateral, your newsletter must serve a clear purpose, and stick to it. The content should all support this overarching purpose, which will ensure the newsletter is a strong communication tool. Is your goal to:

- Provide information?
- Fundraise?
- Recruit new staff?
- Maintain contact with customer base?
- Promote offers and services?
- Drive sales?

Entertain. Make use of a newsletter's informal tone and entertain your reader. Add content from external sources, including humorous stories and cartoons that are related to the purpose of your newsletter and the product or service you are offering. This will break up the more serious content.

Write well. If writing is not your strong point, hire a writer to draft your newsletter. This may also be a good idea for busy business owners that struggle to find the time to complete a monthly outreach piece. Make sure you avoid industry jargon, and if you must use it, make sure to define it for your reader.

Deliver Information. It will be clear to the reader if you are sending a newsletter just for the sake of getting your log into their inbox. Make sure that your newsletter provides information that is relevant and useful to the reader. Have something to say that will benefit the reader, even if it is external content like media clips, events, or website links.

Keep it sweet. Short and sweet, that is. No one has time to read exhaustive amounts of copy, no matter how relevant it may seem. Keep the newsletter tight and limited to a few short news items and some information on your offering. Here are a few tips for managing content length:

- Include a summary of the newsletter content at the top
- Provide short summaries of each article, with a link to "read more"
- Make generous use of headlines and sub headlines
- Put concise information in bullet form

Ask them to act. Always provide a call to action, even if it is a subtle one. You are spending time and money to produce a newsletter in efforts to ultimately increase your business. Ask for the sale – just like you would in a brochure or sales letter. Get readers to visit your website, pick up the phone, fill out the registration form, or lend their support.

Let others speak for you. After you spent all that time gathering great testimonials, make sure you put them to use! If you choose not to dedicate an entire section of your newsletter to customer testimonials, make sure you include them in the header, footer, or margins of the page. They also work well to break up sections of text.

Give it a name. Just like a newspaper, give your newsletter a title that readers will remember and connect to your business.

Make it Attractive and Easy to Read

While content is the backbone of your newsletter, appearance has the ability to engage readers and attract new subscribers. It is also a key factor in the readability of your content, which can make or break a solid readership. Stick to these guidelines for success.

Avoid clutter. Keep the layout clean and free of clutter. Overuse of bright colors and images will distract the reader from your well-crafted content. Use design to enhance your words, not detract from them. Simple design also makes template creation easy.

Make use of headlines and bullets. Make your newsletter easy to scan. Give each column a headline and use bullets to highlight important points. Use sub headlines for important paragraphs, and important testimonials to break up lengthy copy.

Maintain brand consistency. Your newsletter should follow your brand guidelines for elements like color, font, and logo placement. Even if your newsletter is electronic, it is important for each piece of marketing collateral to have a consistent look and feel.

Maintain overall consistency. Once you have designed a newsletter template, stick with it. Each issue should have the same overall look and feel, with only minor modifications if required for image placement, etc. This ensures the newsletter looks professional and readers will learn to recognize it when they receive it.

Use images generously. Images are a powerful way to communicate with an audience and illustrate the words on the page. Pictures, graphs, sidebars or callouts, charts and other graphic elements should be used wherever possible in the newsletter.

Commit to a Timeframe You can Maintain

Choose a frequency you can maintain. Newsletters can be time consuming, so be realistic about how often you promise to distribute them. This depends on your resources, and the needs of your business, but generally once a month to once every three months is a good time frame.

Sending out a newsletter too often can be just as detrimental as not sending them often enough.

When you determine the frequency of your newsletters establish a publishing schedule and stick to it. Work your way into your customer's routine so they are expecting and looking forward to receiving your newsletter.

Develop a publication plan in advance, planning the general themes, overall look and feel, as well as worthy content that will engage your readers will create a loyal following.

Newsletter Content Ideas

- **Company News**

  You may not think so, but your clients and customers are interested in short bits of news about your company and its people. They want to hear about your accolades and successes, since they have helped you achieve them. They are equally interested in reading about the expansion and development of your business, as they have contributed to that growth.

- **Feature Product**

  A feature product or service column is a great way to profile new products or shine a light on existing products that you sell. Use this space to provide an image of the product, and list both benefits and features. Ensure that your feature product is reduced in price to encourage customers to visit your store and purchase it.

- **Employee Profile**

    Just as readers are interested in your company, they are equally interested in the people who work at your company. Profiles of new or recognized employees help to build relationships and establish trust. Your customers will connect the face on the newsletter, to the face that is helping them find what they are looking for, and ultimately close the sale.

- **Cartoons**

    Cartoons in good humor that relate to your business or service can go a long way – literally. If readers find the image funny, there's a good chance they'll forward the newsletter to their friends and family, which means your message has a further reach. Using humor in your newsletter also helps to keep the tone light and informal, showing that you don't take yourself too seriously.

- **Testimonials / Stories**

    A box or column featuring testimonials of the month or a customer story can be an engaging element of your newsletter. People are naturally curious to read about others' experiences and thoughts about consumer products and services. Testimonials are a great way for customers to hear the benefits and praises of your product from someone else.

- **Events**

    If your business hosts regular customer events and seminars, include the pertinent information in your newsletter in a prominently featured events section. Alternately, if your business is an active community participant, consider featuring upcoming community events that you are either sponsoring or attending. Including this kind of information can encourage readers to hang on to the newsletter as a "save the date" piece. If you choose to feature community events, do so strategically. If you cannot include *all* community events, you may create a problem for yourself.

- **Expert Corner (Internal or External)**

    This is one of the greatest added value components of your newsletter: your knowledge and expertise. If relevant to your business, include a column that provides information to your readers from an expert source: either you, or someone you have asked to contribute their knowledge. Doing so will position your company as an expert in your industry and give your reader another reason to hang on to the newsletter. Keep the content relevant – both to your business and current events.

- **Special Offers**

    A newsletter is a great way to inform your readers of special offers and sales. Always include the regular price, or total cost of a package, as well as a high-quality image. If you do not regularly offer discounts, ensure the reader is aware that this is a rare event.

Distributing Your Newsletter

There are essentially two ways to produce your newsletter: print (hard-copy) or electronic (online or email based). Each feature a variety of distribution options.

Take some time to consider your target market, and how they prefer to be communicated with. For example, if your market is teenagers and young adults, electronic newsletters distributed over email may be the most effective. If you focus on reaching seniors, then printed newsletters with large type are best sent via US mail.

Print

Printed newsletters are becoming more and more rare as the popularity of email communication increases. Consumers are also becoming more environmentally conscious and are not interested in receiving stacks of paper in the mail.

Of course, there are plenty of opportunities to use printed newsletters in your businesses. Generally, it is a good idea to produce a printed newsletter and have it available in your business, and when you are on the road, to distribute to potential clients and customers who may not be on your mailing list.

Create a list of the places you will likely wish to distribute your newsletter and produce just enough to satisfy that requirement. The worksheet on the next page will get you started.

Print Newsletter Distribution List

Location	Quantity
☐ Sales Calls	
☐ Presentations	
☐ Meetings	
☐ Trade Shows	
☐ Media Kits	
☐ In-Store	
☐	
☐	
☐	
☐	
☐	
☐	
☐	
☐	
☐	
☐	
☐	
☐	
☐	
☐	
☐	
☐	
☐	
☐	
☐	
☐	
☐	
☐	
☐	
☐	
☐	
☐	
☐	
☐	

Online or Email Newsletters

The most popular newsletters are sent online using Customer Relations Management (CRM) tools in HTML format. There are several CRM tools available online, which charge a monthly subscription fee that is customized to the size of your distribution list, and the frequency of your distribution.

Some common programs are:

- Constant Contact www.constantcontact.com
- Aweber www.aweber.com
- i-contact www.icontact.com
- Campaign Monitor www.campaignmonitor.com

These email marketing programs provide easy to use templates that allow you to design a clean professional email and send it out to your entire contact list.

The benefit of using online tools is that they automatically manage and track the success of each newsletter campaign, including:

- Tracking who opens the email
- Recording what links readers click on
- Tracking how many forwards it to friends
- Unsubscribing those who request it

These tools can also be integrated into your website, so visitors can sign up directly at your site, and begin receiving newsletters immediately.

If you choose not to use a CRM tool, here are a few tips for emailing customers directly:

- **Use the BCC field.** Respect the privacy of your customers and ensure all email addresses are typed into the "BCC" field of your email, not the "To" field. Failing to do so means that everyone on your list will be able to see which email addresses you have on your list. If competitors have subscribed to your newsletter, they will be able to grab the email addresses of your valued customers.

- **No attachments.** Emails from unknown or commercial sources that have attachments are rarely opened. If you create your newsletter on your website in HTML format, you can send a brief note with the website address link to point readers in the right direction.

- **Use plain text.** Make it easy for the reader to open and read your newsletter. Depending on the email program, your formatting may or may not be preserved on the reader's end. If visuals are important to you, the best way to preserve formatting is to use an HTML based template.

- **Keep the old ones!** Remember to post archived newsletters on your site, so readers can catch up on what you've published before they signed up.

To learn how to avoid the 3 key mistakes all small business owners make, visit www.divineresultsbusinessacademy.com

Staying The Course...

It was the great Albert Einstein that once said, "Try not to be a person of success, but rather try to become a person of value." Our goals, dreams, and aspirations have a funny way of revealing who we really are. Always remember that your choices affect not only you but also the ones you love. Unfortunately, we will never be able to appreciate the full consequences of our actions until it is too late. Whatever you aspire to do or become, always think about ways you can add value to the lives of the people around you, especially the ones you love. Knowing that you are working towards your goals not only for you but for the benefit of others as well is one of the biggest motivating factors.

Keeping yourself motivated requires that you create the best possible environment for yourself. This involves surrounding yourself with the kind of people who will lovingly support your dreams or help you develop the skills and gain the knowledge you need to achieve them. Keeping yourself motivated also requires that you take the best possible care of yourself.

You cannot expect to achieve optimal results if your body is being fed mediocre food and getting insufficient rest. Your thoughts also have a powerful effect on your ability to achieve your goals. The fear of failure can immobilize you and bring your pursuit of success to a complete halt. In effect, become so motivated that you condition your mind to keep pushing forward no matter what obstacles come your way.

Becoming successful in any field is going to be a lot of hard work. The system we live in wasn't designed to make us successful people. That is why the world is filled with people who are too afraid to pursue their dreams. These are the same people who will seek to discourage you from pursuing your own dreams as well. I cannot emphasize enough that success, like motivation, is an inside job. It's a mindset.

You must always keep your aspirations in front of you and constantly revise your strategy in order to reach your goals. Once you are motivated to pursue a goal, you will never be satisfied until you accomplish it. That insatiable desire for success is what will propel you to move forward. But this desire will only come about if you learn to define success on your own terms. Always remember that none of us were born to be ordinary!

To learn how to avoid the 3 key mistakes all small business owners make, visit
www.divineresultsbusinessacademy.com

So, What Are Your Next Steps?

A pathway to GREATER success is yours for the taking...Take Action NOW! If you're already an accomplished business owner and earning in excess of $250,000.00 per year, use this book as direction to enhance the speed of your business success. If you are not as accomplished as you would like to be then the smartest thing to do is...

1. Define what has been your profit margin goals?
2. From reading my book, what changes can you make NOW that will cause a noticeable increase over the next 7 days?
3. Have you spoken with your current customer base lately? What are their current needs? What changes have taken place in their lives that your product or service can serve? If nothing else, customer service is vital!
4. Own IT...Results takes place NOW!

Concentrate on strategies to LEARN and the EARN will follow! If you are serious about taking the next step then go to work on yourself, study what other business owners have done to achieve success, understand marketing strategies and become a sponge for new (proven) material. The amazing thing about the game of business is that when you put proven processes to work and continue to follow them, an abundance of success will follow. The biggest mistake is to start a process and then fallback into a vicious never-ending cycle of old habits and limiting beliefs after a short period.

Above all, get the knowledge you need before you step onto the field. If you are a speaker, know your audience; product or service to offer, know your niche market's hot buttons; been a while sense you conducted a product review, start one now; learn the facts. It is amazing to me how many new small business people start the game of business against seasoned professionals (the competition), without first developing the necessary knowledge to be successful. Then they fail and blame the market, the economy, their location, etc.

If you have a business and have not yet managed to start to create wealth and systems that allow you to take time off, build retirement accounts or pay for your children's college, then learn and master the steps outlined in my book. I am a huge advocate of education and mentorships. Get the right information, find someone that knows how to walk you through them and watch your quality of life take a new direction.

To learn how to avoid the 3 key mistakes all small business owners make, visit www.divineresultsbusinessacademy.com